Praise for
The Chinese Century

"Today, there are few places in the world more interesting, intriguing, or important to business than China. Understanding the nuances of conducting business in this fascinating country can make the difference between great success or disappointing failure. Dr. Oded Shenkar shares his valuable insights accumulated over the past 30 years of studying the Chinese business environment. This is a must read for anyone looking to prosper in this important economy."

> Christopher M. Connor
> Chairman and CEO,
> The Sherwin-Williams Company

"For those of us who have lived and worked in Greater China during the last decade, Prof. Shenkar's work realistically captures the sense of momentum, complexity and historical context that underpins China's contemporary ascendancy as a global economic and political force."

> Carl F. Kohrt
> President and CEO,
> Battelle

"The phoenix-like rise of the New Middle Kingdom is and will continue to challenge the political and business landscape of this century. Dr. Shenkar lays out in very readable terms how to remain competitive in the era of this very large tiger. A must read for anyone in politics or business who is involved with long-term strategy."

> James G. (Jim) Oates
> President Emeritus,
> Leo Burnett Company, Inc.

"China is emerging as a dominant global player and every business person will be impacted by its evolution. In The Chinese Century, Oded Shenkar has given us great insights into the changes taking place right before our eyes. This book is a "must read" for every business leader who desires to be successful in the 21st century."

> Lionel Nowell
> Senior VP/Treasurer,
> Pepsico Inc.

"Just what has been needed—a multi-dimensional (across-time, across-geography, and across-industry) view of China's role, and our need to be pro-active in shaping our joint future."

> Keith Davey
> Director, Business Strategy, Asia Pacific & Africa
> and Director, China Business Studies,
> Ford Motor Company (Dearborn, Michigan)

Ideas. Action. Impact.
Wharton School Publishing

In the face of accelerating turbulence and change, business leaders and policy makers need new ways of thinking to sustain performance and growth.

Wharton School Publishing offers a trusted source for stimulating ideas from thought leaders who provide new mental models to address changes in strategy, management, and finance. We seek out authors from diverse disciplines with a profound understanding of change and its implications. We offer books and tools that help executives respond to the challenge of change.

Every book and management tool we publish meets quality standards set by The Wharton School of the University of Pennsylvania. Each title is reviewed by the Wharton School Publishing Editorial Board before being given Wharton's seal of approval. This ensures that Wharton publications are timely, relevant, important, conceptually sound or empirically based, and implementable.

To fit our readers' learning preferences, Wharton publications are available in multiple formats, including books, audio, and electronic.

To find out more about our books and management tools, visit us at whartonsp.com and Wharton's executive education site, exceed.wharton.upenn.edu.

The Chinese Century

*The Rising Chinese Economy and
Its Impact on the Global Economy,
the Balance of Power, and Your Job*

Oded Shenkar

Wharton
UNIVERSITY *of* PENNSYLVANIA

Wharton School Publishing

A CIP record of this book can be obtained from the Library of Congress
LOC Number: 2004106546

Publisher: Tim Moore
Editorial Assistant: Richard Winkler
Marketing Manager: Martin Litkowski
International Marketing Manager: Tim Galligan
Managing Editor: Gina Kanouse
Senior Project Editor: Sarah Kearns
Copy Editor: Karen Gill
Senior Compositor: Gloria Schurick
Indexer: Julie Kawabata
Proofreader: Andrew Wahnsiedler
Cover Design: Chuti Prasertsith
Manufacturing Buyer: Dan Uhrig

Ideas. Action. Impact.
Wharton School Publishing

© 2005 Pearson Education, Inc.
Publishing as Wharton School Publishing
Upper Saddle River, NJ 07458

Wharton School Publishing offers discounts on this book when ordered in quantity for bulk purchases and special sales. For more information, please contact:
U.S. Corporate and Government Sales
(800) 382-3419
corpsales@pearsontechgroup.com

For sales outside of the U.S., please contact:
International Sales
international@pearsoned.com

Company and product names mentioned herein are the trademarks or registered trademarks of their respective owners.

Printed in the United States of America

Sixth Printing

ISBN 0-13-146748-4

Pearson Education Ltd.
Pearson Education Australia Pty., Limited
Pearson Education Singapore, Pte. Ltd.
Pearson Education North Asia Ltd.
Pearson Education Canada, Ltd.
Pearson Educación de Mexico, S.A. de C.V.
Pearson Education—Japan
Pearson Education Malaysia, Pte. Ltd.

Ideas. Action. Impact.
Wharton School Publishing

C. K. Prahalad
THE FORTUNE AT THE BOTTOM OF THE PYRAMID
Eradicating Poverty Through Profits

Yoram (Jerry)Wind, Colin Crook, with Robert Gunther
THE POWER OF IMPOSSIBLE THINKING
Transform the Business of Your Life and the Life of Your Business

Scott A. Shane
FINDING FERTILE GROUND
Identifying Extraordinary Opportunities for New Ventures

Dedication

To the memory of my parents, Bluma and Joshua Shenkar; and to my family, Miriam, Keshet, Joshua, and Rakefet.

Contents

Acknowledgments

Writing a book is a professional and personal challenge, perhaps more so when the topic at hand is close to your heart. China has never ceased to fascinate me, as did reactions from politicians, business people, workers, and academics around the world that over the three decades of my "China watching" shifted from indifference to curiosity and now to enthusiasm—or alarm. In this book, I have tried, and hopefully succeeded, in putting "the China debate" in context. In so doing, I was fortunate to obtain the views, insights, and advice of many individuals in China, the United States, and elsewhere, for which I am grateful. While it is impossible to mention all, I would like to note Dan Chow, who introduced me to the legal aspects of product piracy, and Brian Renwick, who together with a number of anonymous reviewers was instrumental in setting the record straight when my enthusiasm got in the way. At Wharton Publishing, Tim Moore has been the driving force behind the book, from a concept to a finished product. Sarah Kearns has been a wonderful production editor, with endless patience for the "technologically challenged." Martin Litkowski of Pearson, John Grimaldi of the Dilenschneider Group, and Laura Bowers at the Fisher College have all been very helpful in getting the word out. The Dean of the Fisher College, Joe Alutto, the Chairman of the MHR Department, David Greenberger, and Steve Hills and Cheryl Ryan at the CIBER office have all been helpful in providing me with the right work environment.

Last but not least, my family. My wife Miriam has not only put up with my China interests but has been a source of professional and personal inspiration. My children Keshet and Joshua helped me see China through a teenager's and a child's eye, while younger Rakefet (Riki) keeps me focused on the future, in China and beyond. My love and gratitude goes to them all.

About the Author
Oded Shenkar

Oded Shenkar is Ford Motor Company Chair in Global Business Management and Professor of Management and Human Resources at the Fisher College of Business, the Ohio State University. Dr. Shenkar studied China for more than thirty years and has published numerous articles and books on China-related topics, among them *Organization and Management in China 1979-1990* and *International Business in China* (with L. Kelley). He serves on the editorial boards of the *Academy of Management Executive*, the *Journal of Cross-Cultural Management*, the *Journal of International Business Studies*, *Management International Review*, *Human Relations and Organization Studies*, among others, and is Consulting Editor to *Management and Organization Review*, the journal of the International Association for Chinese Management Research.

Dr. Shenkar advises multinational firms as well as start-up enterprises in the United States, the EU, China, Japan, and South Korea, among others. He has also worked with national and state governments as well as with international organizations. He is a Fellow of the Academy of International Business and a member of the Conference Board Council of Integration Executives. He holds B.A. and MSc degrees from the Hebrew University in East Asian Studies and Sociology and M Phil and PhD degrees from Columbia University, New York.

I

The Dawn of the Chinese Century

Economists and editorial writers often paint China's ascent as one more case of an emerging economy on its way up, preceded by Japan and the Asian "tigers" (South Korea, Singapore, Taiwan, and Hong Kong), and soon to be joined by India. It is anything but: China's rise has more in common with the rise of the United States a century earlier than with the progress of its modern-day predecessors and followers. What we are witnessing is the sustained and dramatic growth of a future world power, with an unmatched breadth of resources, lofty aspirations, strong bargaining position, and the financial and technological wherewithal of an established and business-savvy Diaspora. The impact of a rising China on the countries of the world—both developed and developing—will be enormous, and so will be the need to develop strategies and responses to meet the challenge.

This book is not about China bashing in the tradition of the Japan-bashing media of the 1980s, nor a glowing praise of the "Japan as Number 1" genre. Rather, its aim is to capture the impact that the inevitable ascent of China will have on businesses, employees, and consumers around the world—especially in the United States—and assess what firms and individuals will have to do to remain competitive in the new order. It is the position of this book that the "dislocations" brought about by China's advance are not cyclical and temporary but represent fundamental restructuring of the global business system and a repositioning of its key constituencies. We are about to wake up to a new business environment, with new ground rules for business competition, fresh terms of employment, and novel consumption patterns—one that will redraw the battle lines on the political, economic, and social fronts, and one that will place new challenges at the doorstep of nations, firms, and individuals.

China in the Global Economy

If you adjust for purchasing power differentials, China is already the world's second largest economy. Growing at a faster clip than any other major nation, it is on course to surpass the United States as the world's largest economy within two decades. Some observers discount the Chinese growth numbers as exaggerated, but shaving a point, as they suggest, of a GDP growth rate of seven to eight percent would still leave China with the most rapid growth rate in either the developed or developing world over a sustainable time period. Other observers, relying on proxies such as energy consumption, argue that China's growth rate is actually higher than the official numbers suggest. While the Chinese economy faces some serious roadblocks, such as a crumbling banking system, an inefficient service sector, and a significant disenfranchised element, these obstacles are more likely to slow rather than stop China's economic march.

In many industries, especially those that are labor intensive, China is by now the dominant global player. China-based factories make 70 percent of the world's toys, 60 percent of its bicycles, half its shoes, and one-third of its luggage. In those product categories, it is often impossible to find a non-Chinese product on store shelves. In some other product categories, such as textiles and garments, China's share has been held back by quota and tariff walls that are scheduled to come down following the country's accession to the World Trade Organization (WTO) and the expiration of international trade regimes. China, though, is not content with remaining a low-tech, labor-intensive manufacturer. It is already active in areas where technology plays an important role and labor is not the dominant cost factor. The country builds half of the world's microwave ovens, one-third of its television sets and air conditioners, a quarter of its washers, and one-fifth of its refrigerators; these products represent the fastest-growing segment of its exports. Manufacturers in other countries increasingly rely on Chinese components or subassemblies to stay competitive.

Unlike Japan and Korea, China will not let go of the labor-intensive segment as it moves up the ladder. Instead, it will leverage its dominance in labor-intensive and mid-technology industries to fund a major push into knowledge-intensive areas that will drive the future world economy. It is this combined push that will catapult China into the ranks of leading economic powers, and it is this blend that will pose unprecedented challenges to its global competitors. With an increasingly assertive foreign policy, China is also determined to translate its growing economic muscle into geo-political stature and counterbalance what it sees as America's global hegemony. At the same time, like other nations, China will pull its growing political weight in promoting its economic interests.

Resources and Capabilities

The resources that China brings to the table are all too often discounted and misunderstood. To say that this is a country of 1.3 billion people has become some sort of a cliché, until one considers the implications of this enormous size. Foreign firms salivated for years at the thought of selling a toothbrush to every Chinese, a delusion and a symbol of corporate utopia when it first emerged in the early 1980s, but increasingly a reality, even if confined by region or product category. China is already the largest market for Boeing's commercial aircraft and American machine tool makers, and its automotive market is the most promising in the world. (China is already Volkswagen's biggest foreign market, ahead of the United States.)

The attractiveness of its domestic market provides China with tremendous bargaining power, a trump card that was unavailable to Japan and South Korea before it. The lure of its domestic market enables China to require technology transfer as a condition for foreign investor entry, wringing unprecedented concessions. In the automotive industry, foreign firms such as General Motors agreed to establish research and development centers at a scope never before contemplated in a developing market. Not only did these manufacturers agree to transfer technology that is arguably close to their core capabilities, but they consented to do so in an environment with virtually no protection of intellectual property rights (IPR) and in parallel alliances never before seen: China is the only country in the world where domestic automotive makers maintain equity ventures with competing foreign partners, which makes it possible to learn "best practices" from both and end up with potentially more knowledge than either foreign party. The aim is to produce Chinese multinationals that will hold their own in a global economy and replicate the success of Toyota, Sony, and Samsung, but in a shorter time frame.

China's size also means a vast pool of human resources. The reservoir includes not only an unlimited supply of menial laborers, but also a large and growing number of engineers, scientists, and skilled technicians, many of whom are employed in government-funded research and development centers or in the increasingly prominent technological centers established by foreign multinationals. The coexistence of cheap labor with increasingly abundant skilled personnel defies common assumptions on national competitiveness as a case of "either or" and underlies China's strategy of sustaining its dominance in labor-intensive industries even as it enters technology-intensive realms.

China's scope and pace of modernization of its own educational system is much greater than that of earlier contenders. Even today, Japan's educational system remains largely insular to foreign influences as well as to change in general, which is something the Japanese acknowledge as a serious obstacle to economic advancement and growth in a knowledge economy. Korean universities, while more open than their Japanese counterparts, have only recently started to actively recruit overseas faculty, although they have been recruiting Korean nationals educated abroad for years. Chinese institutions of higher education are showing more openness, and at least the elite institutions are displaying not only readiness but also enthusiasm for adjusting curriculum and making other changes. China's top universities are moving aggressively to upgrade their infrastructure and skill sets, establishing alliances with Western institutions and companies and actively courting foreign-trained faculty.

In addition to boosting its own educational system, China is counting on an eventual influx of Chinese students returning from abroad. Chinese students are now the largest contingent of foreign students in the United States. According to the Institute of International Education, more than 64,000 students from mainland China studied in the United States in 2002–2003. In the same year, the U.S. also hosted more than 8,000 students from Hong Kong and more than 28,000 from Taiwan, for a total of over 100,000. Chinese students also study in Europe, Australia, and Japan, among other host countries. The Chinese government has been accelerating its efforts to entice the best and brightest of this crop to return, offering "overseas terms" and joint appointments to the most promising prospects. Even without formal incentives, many students as well as practicing scientists and executives are lured back by the wealth of economic opportunities offered by a fast growing economy. These returnees are bringing with them not only academic knowledge, but also something else the Chinese sorely need: application know-how and business-related expertise.

Another important source of technological, scientific, and managerial knowledge resides in the economies of Taiwan and Hong Kong. Pushed in part by Chinese low-end producers breathing at their necks, both territories—not to mention Singapore—have been busy upgrading their educational systems over the past two decades. Hong Kong now boasts eight universities, up from three in the late 1970s. These universities, some of which are world class, play a key role in upgrading China's human resource infrastructure; increasingly, they are host to mainland students, and many of their local graduates end up working directly or indirectly with mainland enterprises.

That said, China has a long way to go before it can overcome key weaknesses, such as lacking a developed service sector to support its manufacturing base and to which to channel some of its superfluous personnel, a banking sector not far from default, and a limited ability to generate technological innovation. Judging from past experience, however, there is every reason to believe that China will be able to overcome these problems, emerging even stronger from the process. A key strength is that China is not alone; rather, it's the hub of a cluster of complementary and increasingly integrated economies that is Greater China.

The Synergies of Greater China

In a cultural, economic, and geo-political sense, China consists not only of the People's Republic, but also of Hong Kong, an entrepreneurial center which, from 1997, has been a Special Administrative Region of China with its own trade and foreign investment jurisdiction; Taiwan, a technologically advanced island, its contentious political status notwithstanding (China sees Taiwan as a renegade province), which is increasingly integrated into the Chinese economy; perhaps even predominantly Chinese Singapore, a center for high technology manufacturing and a base for many multinational enterprises; and a vast Chinese Diaspora that occupies the ranks of much of the business elites of Southeast Asia and is active in business circles around the globe. An example is Hong Kong-based Hutchison Whampoa, a diversified conglomerate with close to $20 billion in revenue and operations in more than 40 countries.

Put these different parts of the Chinese puzzle together, and you find unequaled potential: a human resource pool that is not only the largest in the world but also includes a large number of scientists, engineers, and seasoned executives; an advanced and rapidly progressing technological infrastructure, and a leading industry position in many emerging technologies (Taiwan is the world's largest producer of notebook computers); vast capital (together, the economies of China, Taiwan, Hong Kong, and Singapore have three-quarter trillion dollars in foreign reserves); a dominant trade position (Hong Kong's container port is among the busiest and most advanced in the world); major bases and Asian regional headquarters for multinational enterprises (Shanghai, Hong Kong, and Singapore); and global business savvy (the Chinese Diaspora).

Increasingly integrated (Singapore somewhat less so) and dependent on their mainland China business, those economies possess complementary and synergetic attributes of capital, skill, knowledge, human resources, and market savvy that can deliver development on a magnitude and at a pace never before seen in a developing economy. At almost $1.4 trillion, Greater China's (the PRC, Hong Kong, Taiwan, and Singapore) merchandise trade trails only that of the European Union and the U.S. and is almost double the Japanese volume. In an increasingly global economy, this volume forms the basis for tremendous bargaining power as other trading nations weigh their responses to trade and economic issues in the context of broader flows and their own exports. Greater China is rapidly becoming the hub for an even larger and rapidly growing Asian economy: Mainland China is already South Korea's biggest export market, while Greater China is the biggest market for virtually all other Asian nations.

Coming to America

In the nineteenth century, the West forced a weak China to accept a series of unequal and humiliating treaties, forcing it to open its doors to foreign trade. The United States was a signatory to one of those treaties. The problem was that while the West coveted such Chinese products as tea and silk, it had little to offer in return that the Chinese would want (which is partially how the British got into the opium trade). Close to two centuries later, trade between the former adversaries is booming, and, again, Americans seem more interested in Chinese goods than Chinese are interested in America's. This time around, the Chinese want to sell, and American and European ports handle a lot more made-in-China merchandise than tea and silk.

Exhibit 1-1 displays China's trade in goods and services with the United States. Numbers are provided not only for mainland China (The People's Republic of China, or PRC for short), but also for Greater China (including Hong Kong, Taiwan, and Macao, but not Singapore), both to acknowledge the increased integration of these Chinese economies and to address a major complaint of the U.S. China Business Council, a U.S. trade group consisting of major U.S. exporters to China, that the trade numbers for the PRC are distorted because they do not account for Hong Kong's *entrepôt* position. (That is, many exports coming from the PRC come via Hong Kong, and many U.S. exports with a Hong Kong shipping address are destined for mainland China.) We include services because unlike merchandise trade in which it has a chronic deficit, the United States has a considerable surplus in the trade of services (such as transportation and consulting).

The U.S.-China Business Council also holds that the U.S. trade deficit with China is inflated, because the U.S. calculates imports and exports differently: U.S. imports are measured on a CIF (inclusive of cost, insurance, and freight), while its exports are calculated on an FAS (free alongside ship) basis. The Council contends that conversion of both imports and exports to an FOB (free on board) basis would adjust exports

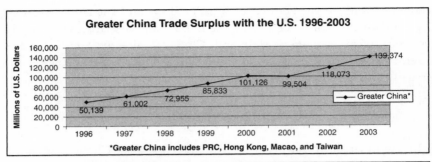

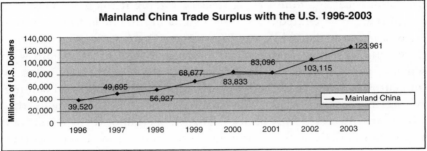

Source: Census Bureau's Foreign Trade (FT-900), U.S. International Trade in Goods and Services annual issues. Updated 5/15/2003.

Exhibit 1-1 China's Balance of Trade with the United States.

upward by 1 percent and reduce imports by as much as 10 percent.[1] Even with such adjustments, China would still post a huge trade surplus with the U.S., and considering the rate of growth for the deficit, the new numbers would merely reflect a six-month time lag. Furthermore, adjusting U.S. trade figures would not alter China's position relatively to other U.S. traders. The defensive position of the U.S.-China Business Council is revealing: It is a reminder of the powerful business lobby for China, which consists of major exporters to this market, such as Boeing, and those who rely on Chinese imports to remain competitive.

No less important than the overall numbers of the trade deficit is the composition of the deficit—in particular, Chinese imports into the United States. According to the Foreign Trade Division of the U.S. Census Bureau, the four highest import categories from China in 2003 were all technology related: miscellaneous manufactured articles at $28.5 billion (CIF value), office machine and automatic data processing equipment at $24.3 billion, telecommunications and sound recording equipment at $17.5 billion, and electrical machinery at $12.6 billion. The labor-intensive categories of apparel/clothing and footwear are in fifth and sixth place, at $12.6 and $11.1 billion respectively, continuing a downward trend in ranking but not volume.[2] In 1999, in comparison, textile and apparel (together) and footwear placed second and third, respectively.

Economists are divided over how important a trade balance is. Some point out that the U.S. trade deficit is not huge as a proportion of GDP, even though it has already crossed five percent, which is an arbitrary red line. Others point out the danger of an increasing proportion of American financial obligations held in the hands of foreigners, who, if they were to lose faith in the American currency, could cause a crisis of confidence in the United States and destabilize a global economy in which the U.S. dollar remains the main reserve currency. It is commonly accepted that trade brings about mutual benefits to trading partners, with some suggesting that trade is beneficial even when not reciprocal (for example, U.S. consumers benefit from cheap Chinese products). An economic perspective is too narrow to capture the complexity of trade, its variable impact on diverse regions and industries, and, in particular, its social, political, and geopolitical repercussions. It is easy to make the macro economic argument that "free trade benefits us all"; it is also easy to make the often-political argument for "fair trade." It is much more difficult to pinpoint the parameters for fairness, identify who is playing fair in a new game, or pick winners (and losers). The China game may redefine all three.

Why is the United States the most vulnerable to (some would say the major beneficiary of) Chinese imports? In contrast to Japan, who for decades maintained a huge trade surplus with the outside world, China has been running only a small surplus in its global trade, and recently its imports have been rising faster than its exports. As its trade surplus with the United States expanded to $11.5 billion in January 2004, China's overall trade balance for February 2004 expanded to $8 billion—in the red. This means that other trading partners are doing quite well, maintaining a smaller deficit (the European Union, or EU) or a substantial surplus (Asia) in their China trade. (With the EU, China had a surplus of close to 50 billion euros in 2002, running a surplus with every EU country with the exception of Austria and Finland.)

How is this disparity between the United States and China's other trade partners possible? The answer is quite complex, as is explaining the variations, say, between the United Kingdom (UK), which proportionally runs an even greater deficit with China, and Germany, whose deficit is relatively small. The explanations are important in that each has its own supporting constituencies, each sheds different light on the China impact, and each offers its own repertoire of strategic responses at the national, industry, firm, and individual levels. The following sections present some of the explanations.

The Chronic Importer

The United States has been running a trade deficit with the rest of the world for a quarter of a century, a gap which now approaches the half a trillion dollar mark annually. Nominally, this is the largest trade deficit in the world, and hovering around 5 percent of GDP, it is also one of the highest ratios among industrialized nations. The U.S. has a substantial trade deficit with the EU, Canada, and Japan, among others, but its trade deficit with China is the largest and the fastest growing. One reason for China's lead is the global shift of manufacturing operations to the country. As Japanese, European, and American firms have been moving their manufacturing operations to China, their sales in the United States register as Chinese exports. For instance, over the past few years, the Japanese trade surplus with the U.S. has not grown, while the deficit with China has soared. Obviously, this argument does not explain why the U.S. overall trade deficit has not declined, which suggests that there may be other factors at play, such as competitiveness, exchange rates, the increasing offerings of global exporters, and the diversity of the U.S. population that supposedly enhances its appetite for foreign goods.

The Naïve Trader (or the One with More to Lose)

The United States is an open market, which many Americans (but not necessarily everyone else) believe has less tariff and nontariff barriers than those of it partners, and trade policies that Americans and many others would characterize as naïve (such as allowing relatively open access to American markets without insisting on reciprocity). In this view, the U.S. is being taken advantage of by its trade partners, especially China. China's defenders point to the gradual opening of its markets and its World Trade Organization (WTO) commitments. They argue, not without justification, that many American firms have not invested the necessary time and energy in understanding the requirements of a rapidly opening Chinese market. Nicholas Lardy, a noted China scholar with the Institute for International Economics, observes that China's ratio of imports to GDP likely reached 30 percent in 2004 compared to 8 percent in Japan and 14 percent in the United States.[3]

As a global leader in technology and innovation and a net technology exporter, the United States can be said to suffer more from China's lax regime of intellectual property protection than other trade partners. Analogies are often drawn with Japan and the "four tigers" that started with disregard for property rights but later enhanced compliance though Chinese violations persist on a much grander scale and are tolerated, often supported and protected by powerful local interests. As China moves up the technology ladder, states the optimistic argument, it will be in its own interest to offer such protection. After all, in the nineteenth century, the United States was a major violator of intellectual property rights, as Charles Dickens, among others, learned to his dismay. The difference is that this time around, the share of research and development in product costs is much higher, and copyrighted products take up much more of the economic pie. We are also in a global economy, meaning that pirated and counterfeit products now find their ways to multiple markets. And, perhaps most worryingly, recent trends show a rise rather than a decline in the rate of violations.

Follow the Curve

In this explanation, the U.S.-China trade imbalance results from the different point of the two countries along the development curve. In the same way that the United States lost agricultural employment a century ago, it is now shedding low-end manufacturing jobs, replacing them with higher-end, knowledge-intensive manufacturing and service jobs. In so doing, China plays a positive role by relieving the United States to do what it does best: producing and implementing knowledge at the upper rung of the ladder. The argument is understandably attractive to China's defenders, who point out that China and the United States overlap only on a narrow range of products (10 percent according to the Council on U.S. China Trade). Naturally, the development curve story implies that the trade gap between the two countries will diminish once China progresses.

The argument is appealing but also vulnerable. The range of products on which the United States and China compete is probably larger than the Council attests, and most importantly, is growing rapidly, which should not be surprising given the faster growth that China has been experiencing and the massive technology transfer into the country. Toyota, Nissan, and Honda started with lower-end vehicles before they established the luxury divisions of Lexus, Infiniti, and Acura; inquiries by the International Trade Commission reveal that Chinese TV sets and furniture already target both the low and high end. The development curve argument typically draws a parallel between economies shifting from manufacturing to services and from agriculture to manufacturing, but as we will argue later in this book, the parallel may be fundamentally flawed. Finally, unlike Japan and the tigers before it, China intends to retain its labor-intensive advantage as it moves into more sophisticated product lines; if it manages to do so, the range of products on which the two countries compete will grow still further.

Foreign-Generated and "Self-Inflicted" Imports

Looking at the trade data, you may see a picture of unscrupulous Chinese firms trying to elbow their way into the U.S. market. Before you jump to conclusions, however, keep in mind that more than half of China's global exports are by foreign multinationals that have set up shop there to supply their home and global markets (see Exhibit 1-2). In fact, the Chinese, like the Japanese before them, tend to subtract such exports from their trade figures, producing much lower export numbers.

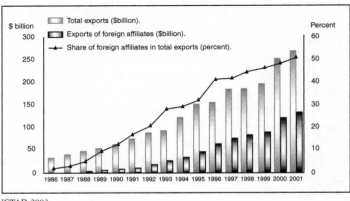

Source: UNCTAD 2003.

Exhibit 1-2 China's Exports and the Share of Foreign Affiliates.

"Foreign Invested Enterprises" (foreign subsidiaries and cross-border joint venture companies) account for a big chunk of China's export growth because they have the know-how, quality level, reputation, distribution channels, and markets necessary for foreign market entry. Many—although by no means all—are American firms, driven by economic fundamentals (that is, it is cheaper to manufacture in China even when you take into account shipping and related costs) or by agreements they have signed with the Chinese government requiring a high export to sales ratio as a condition for domestic market entry or to obtain certain investment incentives. While some dispute the numbers, it is clear that American firms support Chinese imports into the U.S. if not as manufacturers than as buyers (such as Disney). Furthermore, the contribution of U.S. manufacturers to China's exports is likely to grow, and it is easy to see why: China's technology products are the fastest growth segment of its exports, foreign multinationals account for three-quarters of technology exports (more in the case of high technology), and the U.S. remains the largest repository of technological knowledge. And there is one more reason: Compared to other developed economies, in particular the European Union, it is relatively simple to shut down operations in the United States, so manufacturing operations can be moved more easily to China and start exporting back into the U.S. In contrast, EU firms (in particular in Germany and France) face enormous obstacles in shutting down domestic plants, which erode the cost/benefit equation of moving production off-shore and, at least in the short run, reduce exports into the region.

The Currency Play

The almost pathetic view of the U.S. Secretary of the Treasury, John Snow, making a pilgrimage to China to plead for a revaluation of the yuan only to be turned down, focused attention on the role played by the *renminbi* (literally, "people's money") in the trade imbalance between the two countries. Most economists (as well as competitors and developed country unions) are convinced that the yuan is undervalued, although they disagree about the margin as well as on how risky a sudden appreciation would be for China and the global economy. Now that the U.S. dollar has declined against the euro (especially) and the Japanese yen, the pressure is on China to revalue to make Chinese products more expensive in the U.S. market.

The currency game was played vis-à-vis Japan during the 1980s, when, in the wake of the Plaza Accord, the dollar plunged in value against the yen. Yet, the drastic realignment in exchange rates hardly made a dent in the U.S. trade balance with Japan, leading frustrated economists to offer alternative explanations (such as that consumption patterns were not dependent on cost alone) and even to suggest that "Japan does not fit the economic models." Today, the yen is worth more than double its early 1980s dollar value, but the U.S. trade deficit with Japan is still the same (in 1980s dollar terms). Although the deficit would have been higher without the realignment, it was probably held back more by Japanese factories moving to the United States (especially in the case of the automotive industry, which accounts for a big chunk of the U.S. deficit with Japan) and China.

The constituencies pressuring for revaluation would like China to do one of the two: let the yuan free float, thus letting market forces determine exchange rate, or set a new, higher exchange rate band. In the past, China has rejected such pressure as intervening in its internal affairs, reminding everyone how it agreed not to devalue its currency in the face of massive devaluations by competitors such as South Korea, Thailand, and Indonesia during the Asian Financial Crisis. China's offer to use its huge reserves to support the Hong Kong dollar, then under attack, also gives credence to its stance that it will not yield on exchange rate pressures. While giving some signals regarding its future readiness for a modest revaluation, an emerging deficit in its overall trade balance will give China further rationale for opposing a change in current rates. Opposing the yuan revaluation are also the many U.S. manufacturers who import components or finished products from China and would be affected adversely by such change.

China Takes on the World

China's pressure on U.S. markets will only grow stronger. Companies that until now hesitated about shifting production to the country due to union agreements or for fear of a consumer backlash now realize they may have no choice if they wish to stay in business. Firms initially protected from Chinese competition by high transportation costs find themselves on the firing line as logistic costs decline and as productivity rises on the Chinese side. Others are following their industrial customers who have moved to China and need their suppliers and service providers to be close by. Even companies supplying the U.S. defense establishment now realize they may have little choice, although they try hard to keep their core operations at home. Consultants and other service personnel follow to provide support for those operations and discover that China, like some other low-cost nations, is a good base from which to support overseas operations.

"The great and well-known amount of imports of the productions of China into the United States," wrote Daniel Webster, Secretary of State in the John Tyler administration, in 1843, "are not likely to be diminished."[4] Eventually, of course, it did. But while the quote serves as a reminder of the limits of forecasting, indications are that for now, the tide of Chinese exports will only grow. It will also not stop at America's shores. For now, the EU runs a merchandise trade deficit of about $45 billion with China, but imports from China represent merely 1.8 percent of its total imports (EU countries included), and half its volume of Japanese imports (2002 figures). Once Chinese exports grow—and especially when they begin to challenge Europe's strategic and politically influential industries such as motor vehicles—the sentiment may change there, too, although it will remain subdued as long as European exports remain strong and as long as the more influential EU nations, such as Germany, have a relatively small deficit. Japan, whose worries about China are also geo-political, is especially vulnerable to China's ascent, because its competitive advantage lies in manufacturing, its economy has stagnated for over a decade, and its governance and corporate practices have slowed its adjustment to a changing global economy. Like the U.S., Japan's exports to China are about half its import level, and as in the case of the U.S., many of its imports from China are by Japanese firms that now manufacture there. However, unlike in the U.S. case, China is the only major economy with which Japan runs a significant trade deficit (Japan's exports to the U.S. are about twice its import level), which cushions the impact. And, being much more dependent on trade than both the U.S. and China, Japan can ill-afford to challenge the free trade system.

While the industrialized countries take (artificial) solace from the belief that China only threatens the labor-intensive part of their economies, developing nations do not have that luxury. Developing countries find themselves trailing in the contest for developed country investment dollars and watch with trepidation as foreign investors uproot operations in their markets and shift them to China. The Chinese edge in terms of cheaper labor cost, a modern infrastructure, and the benefits of scale and agglomeration is now often sufficient to erase the proximity advantage of countries like Mexico, who have been counting on the combination of geography and NAFTA as a sort of insurance policy in the U.S. market. They are now finding out that payout is not guaranteed.

For emerging and developing economies in Asia, the Chinese impact is more ambivalent. While Asian countries continue to lose foreign investment to their powerful neighbor, the country is becoming an engine of growth for the entire region and a complement if not a substitute to developed country markets. (For instance, China has now replaced the United States as South Korea's largest foreign market.) With the notable exception of Japan, most Asian economies are running a trade surplus with China, and so do not see Chinese imports as an immediate concern. Nevertheless, China is considered a possible worry among Asian nations, some of which are only one step ahead on the development ladder and hence vulnerable to Chinese economic progress. In addition, there is considerable unease about the influence of the Chinese business elite, especially in the Muslim nations of Indonesia and Malaysia, as well as suspicion that the Chinese minority will benefit from China's rise while the ethnic masses will suffer as low-paying jobs move to China. Finally, Asian nations are concerned with changing geopolitics: Post World War II Japan was suspected because of its prewar and war record, but it did not have the military might and was a close U.S. ally. China, while historically nonexpansionist, is still a Communist nation, with the largest standing army in the world and strong geo-political aspirations.

In the heels of the China impact will come numerous aftershocks that will ripple their way throughout the world: rising prices for the energy and commodities that the burgeoning Chinese economy is devouring, severe "dislocations" for employees and their communities in regions and industries unable to compete or restructure, waves of immigrants pushed out of Central America and other regions by the devastation of the labor-intensive operations they have come to rely upon, and, down the road, a new geo-political order in which China takes one of the leadership roles.

The World's Factory

Take a toy into your hands and, more likely than not, it will have a "Made in China" label. This is no surprise: China makes 7 of every 10 conventional toys sold in the world. That seems not to be a concern for the United States, which long ago conceded toy manufacturing to other economies, such as South Korea, Hong Kong, and Taiwan who, in turn, now have to contend with the new boy in town, China. U.S. toy giants such as Hasbro and Mattel remain competitive by moving production to low-cost locations while retaining design, development, and marketing skills in-house, under a powerful brand name. Toy manufacturing uses for the most part rudimentary technology, is not "strategic," and has no national security implications. The same is true for other labor-intensive industries, such as textiles that the United States exited, moved up market, or relied on immigrant labor to prolong its staying power.

China is no longer only about toys, however. Today, it is a major player in product lines that are still mass produced in America and Europe, such as home appliances, and China-made components are used extensively by the competition. The next phase will see subcontracting of entire operations, with the foreign firm maintaining oversight, branding, and marketing. When they export back, however, these established developed country firms will face competition from a new breed of Chinese manufacturers that export under their own brand name and in some instances set up for production on U.S. soil. China is also fast becoming a player in capital-intensive products, such as motor vehicles, as well as in technology-intensive lines, some of which, like flat-screen TV, have conceivable strategic use. Greater China now accounts for more than eight percent of global merchandise exports, with the mainland alone responsible for more than six percent. This may not seem much until you look at the growth curve: In 1996, the figure was less than three percent.

The shift toward China-based manufacturing is also underpinned by impressive advances in global supply chains. Driven by technological improvements and managerial efficiencies, the cost of logistics has been on a downward trend for two decades, and in some cases is down by two-thirds from its level a decade or two ago. The savings lower the cost of importation of finished goods and of components that travel back and forth between China and the United States (although volume increases have upped the cost of shipping from China). Savings also come from improved turnaround time, which is a crucial variable in customized products such as furniture, one of the fastest growing "Made in China" import categories. American imports of Chinese-made furniture and bedding have now exceeded $10 billion, up from less than $4 billion just two years ago.

The Export Imperative

China is still less reliant on exports than many other countries in Asia (such as Malaysia) and outside (such as Belgium), but its dependence is growing, and the export drive must continue for it to fund its growing imports of capital goods and production inputs and prevent a social and political time bomb from exploding, with unemployment serving as the trigger. Not only does China need to provide jobs to a huge cohort of young people, but it also must worry about the many millions still employed in money-losing state enterprises and the 100–200 million people who have left the countryside in search of work in urban areas and who would be the first to be affected by a serious economic downturn. Disaffected peasants have been a source of rebellion throughout Chinese history, and economic well-being is especially critical to a regime that has shed its ideological base and now relies on economic prosperity and nationalism as its sole sources of legitimacy.

Given the scale of its economy and its increased dominance in many product markets, the continuation of China's export drive will bring about commoditization of product markets that have previously relied on brand name and reputation for differentiation. With China as the cost leader, foreign manufacturers will have to meet or beat the Chinese "pricing floor" that rests not only on cheap labor and subsidies, but also on massive use of counterfeiting and piracy to circumvent development costs. This leaves industrialized country manufacturers with a limited range of options. The first option is to procure many if not most of the product's components and subassemblies from a Chinese producer, thus lowering the cost of the final product to the point of remaining competitive. This trend is already in full swing, with U.S. automotive firms sourcing billion of dollars in Chinese parts. The second option is to move operations to China to lower cost further as well as gain entry to the Chinese market. A third option is to find another production base, such as India or Mexico, that can meet or beat Chinese prices, but those locations rarely offer the combined benefits of a China base. A fourth option is to automate or otherwise increase productivity; however, in many traditional product lines, the most obvious productivity savings may have already been extracted; and, with key supporting industries exiting the market, it will be especially difficult to extend or even sustain productivity gains. Finally, firms faced with Chinese competition can shift from the fiercely competitive entry level into technology-intensive product lines, but they will find the steps leading up crowded by their counterparts who have had the same idea. Or, they can exit the business altogether, seeking to redeploy their resources into more promising endeavors.

Where the Jobs Are

Employees in labor-intensive industries, where labor costs represent a significant portion of product cost, are predictably the hardest hit by Chinese competition. Industries like textiles and garments rely on low or minimum wage labor, often done by immigrants from Mexico, Africa, and the Caribbean, yet they cannot compete with wages of barely above 50 cent an hour. With the exception of Bangladesh, Vietnam, and a few others, even developing economies cannot compete with such wages, especially when accompanied by higher productivity and infrastructure advantages. American makers of textile, apparel, and related products have been protected until now by international quota agreements and other tariffs, but those are coming down now. Low transportation cost, quick delivery, and fast reaction to changing consumer tastes are no longer sufficient to shield the industry from Chinese competition even when combined with political pressure on the part of elected officials in affected regions, such as the Carolinas.

China's job impact will not remain confined to labor-intensive industries. As the country moves up the technology ladder, the jobs affected will also be better paying and knowledge based. In the manufacturing sector, white-collar jobs, from accountants to back-office, are especially at risk, as are jobs within the service economy, such as insurance and banking. Although the latter, as well as software, are presently less at risk from China then they are from other countries, from India to Ireland, China is a factor: One reason for India's software push is that it is one of the few sectors where it is globally competitive vis-à-vis China, and even that edge may come under pressure as China upgrades its educational system.

The Chinese market is also creating many jobs for those industries that export their goods and services to China. China is the fastest growing U.S. export market; however, the magnitude and the composition of the U.S. trade deficit with China suggests that the number of jobs created there by exports to America is much higher than the number of jobs owing their existence to U.S. exports to China. Further, the job gains and the job losses are in different regions, industries, sectors, and company types. The variable impact is, in turn, laying the ground for conflict and misalignment of interests between winners and losers in this round of the trade game.

A Consumer Paradise

China has helped create what seems like a shoppers' paradise in the U.S., as well as in other countries. Many of the product lines that China now dominates, like wristwatches and bicycles, experienced an unprecedented real price decline. This has been good news for consumers. The commoditization of previously branded products has brought into the market consumers who in the past could not afford the product and enabled others to shift portions of their disposable income toward the purchase of higher level or a broader array of products and services, including those domestically made. At the same time, the flood of Chinese imports is creating unprecedented pressures on manufacturers who rely on brand name or country-of-origin impact (such as Italian leather goods), especially for below-luxury products, which were already pressured by the expansion of large discounters.

The growth of Chinese products on American store shelves is related closely to the rise of discounters like Wal-Mart, for whom China is progressively becoming the cornerstone in a strategy of offering the lowest possible prices for broad merchandise offerings. Wal-Mart, like other discount retailers, is becoming more and more dependent on China to provide offerings at "can't be beat" prices. The relation is symbiotic: China is dependent on Wal-Mart and like retailers to gain market entry for its yet-unknown brands by leveraging the retailer's name and huge scale. The cooperation is helping Wal-Mart solidify its position as the largest retailer in the world, while enabling Chinese firms produce to scale, which is a critical variable in mass-produced merchandise.

China's ascent may have broader consequences for the American consumer and, by the extension, for the U.S.' social and political landscape. Until now, complaints by manufacturing employees that the purchase of foreign products was undermining their livelihood, and hence the livelihood of other Americans whose products they would not be able to purchase once they were out of a job, fell on deaf ears. As long as the economy was quick to recover and create jobs, it was easy to sidestep the negative sentiment by showing the benefits of an open trade system for job creation and wealth. This time around, there seems to be at best an unexpected lag in job creation and at worst a structural change limiting job creation. With programs devised to handle the plight of trade losers lagging behind, the atmosphere is changing even if trade is only one factor contributing to job losses. Politicians are catching up with the new sentiment, and consumers may, too.

The Chinese challenge is of a magnitude that may alter the purchase equation, igniting a "buy American" debate. This could fundamentally change purchasing choices, replacing a cost/reputation formula with one incorporating job preservation as a key consideration. American consumers are said to prefer foreign brands, a preference used as one explanation for the huge trade deficit. Consumers have been willing to pay a premium for European and Japanese brands even under seemingly identical quality with U.S. brands. (Note, for instance, the premium that customers pay for the Toyota product versus the GM vehicle coming out of the same joint venture factory.) However, as the recent drop in French wine consumption following the Iraq war suggests, American consumers do not lack the ability to link their purchasing decisions with geopolitics, animosity perceptions, and other "nonrational" considerations. These considerations may yet come to occupy center stage in a fiercely contested consumer market.

The Coming Realignment

China's ascent will bring about novel challenges to "common wisdoms" and rethinking of old terms and assumptions anchored in events past. How do you classify a country governed by a Communist regime but whose government share of GDP is less than half that of the U.S.? An economy that attracts the largest volume of foreign investment in history without providing adequate protection for intellectual property rights? One with extremely high savings rates but which grossly misallocates investment capital? One with the most competitive market in certain segments, but which has a paternalistic subsidy regime? A stabilizing force in world affairs that is now threatening the use of force to regain its "renegade province" of Taiwan? China will challenge these and many other dichotomies we have come to accept; it may also realign the economic, political, and social landscape in the United States as well as in other countries. Among the coming impacts and challenges in the United States:

- An increasing fault line separating those U.S. industries and firms who see themselves as primarily beneficiaries of an increasing China trade and investment and those who see themselves as victims of China's ascent. The first group consists of multinationals with extensive China operations; the second includes companies who cannot substitute China investment for exit, including many small and medium firms. The two groups will take on an opposing position on trade and protectionism and may align with the two political parties on the basis of their trade agenda.

- A return of job security to center stage of employer-employee negotiations and a possible reversal of a decade-old trend away from unionization. The feeling of vulnerability now grappling sectors that until recently saw themselves immune to off-shore job loss might entice the unionization of high-skill knowledge workers and bring about significant changes in the structure of the union movement and its activities.

- Severe pressures toward protectionism not seen for 70 years or so, including not only pressure to establish temporary tariffs, but also demands for renegotiation of trade agreements and challenges to the role of international institutions, most notably the WTO. With increasing concerns about the U.S. being the loser in the trade game, the risk of protectionism and its heavy damage to the global economy looms larger than ever.

- Paraphrasing the trade debate in terms of "rational economics" versus "hot-headed protectionism" will no longer do. While the benefits of free trade are clear, the long-term realities of a service-based economy lacking a manufacturing base are nothing but. The same is true for the assumption that the U.S. economy can prosper by continuing to be the global innovator and focus on added value economic activities in a world where most nations aspire to, and invest in, the same strategy; and for the belief that the United States can indefinitely absorb the world's output paid for by U.S. assets.

For companies, employees, and consumers, the question is no longer if and when China is coming, for it is already here, but how to prepare for the new economy. Side by side the new economic realities, a new geo-political order is being created. For instance, seeing the length to which the United States and Europe went to secure their oil reserves, why wouldn't an energy-starved and increasingly assertive China take the same route? And why wouldn't it leverage its economic muscle for geo-political gains through such means as economic assistance, training, and defense support? For all the similarities, millennia of Chinese history suggest that it will chart its own course, but if history is clue (and I believe it is), China will not be satisfied with anything but a position of prominence, however defined.

So where does all this leave us? First, there is the unsettling prospect of a trade war. In an age of global interdependence, protectionism will be a severe mistake, producing grave consequences for all; yet this is where we may be heading if we continue to hold on to old clichés and false analogies—like the one asserting that the current shift from manufacturing to services is a repeat of the move from agriculture to manufacturing a century ago—until they hit a reality wall. Second, we share the responsibility of maintaining the perception of fairness, which lies at the heart of the American psyche. If we fail to identify and assist the losers in this new round of the trade game, the belief in opportunity for all may be undermined, and with it, the broad participation that makes America what it is: a haven for the openness and innovativeness but with a sense of inclusion. The challenge is how to do so without infringing on the dreams and hopes of other constituencies in the global economy, both at home and abroad. While we continue to look for the balance, the more immediate question for both firms and individuals is not how to stop the tide of Chinese imports, but how to remain competitive in the dawning Chinese century. That is what this book is about.

2

The Middle Kingdom

China's extensive history casts a long shadow over its present handling of business, science, and economy. As chaotic and rapidly changing as China's economic and business scene may seem, it is deeply anchored in past traditions and their perceived lessons and marks. Understanding this past is vital because it sheds light on what we see today and, perhaps more importantly, may provide essential clues regarding China's future course: the scope and level of its aspirations and the policies and strategies that are likely to be adopted to get it there.

Three periods stand out as key milestones in China's rich and long history:

- The Imperial period, which lasted intermittently for more than two millennia
- The partially overlapping "foreign humiliation" period of the nineteenth and early twentieth centuries
- The three early decades of Communist rule from 1949 up to the launch of the reforms in late 1978, including the first years of reforms that followed

These three periods alternate as yardsticks for achievement and reminders of hardship, failure, and errors to be avoided if past glory is to be restored. The Imperial period, officially repudiated by the Communist regime as feudal and exploitative, nevertheless remains a benchmark for national grandeur. The encounter and conflict with the West in the nineteenth and twentieth centuries serve mostly as a reminder of the humiliation suffered by a militarily weak and technologically backward China and impact current attitudes toward foreign investment and scientific progress. The central planning legacy of the early decades of Communist rule is a celebration of the restoration of national dignity as much as a focal point from which to reflect on the deficiencies of a rigid economic system. These three periods remain in the collective psyche, impacting the political and economic aspirations of the Chinese leadership, its policies and strategies, and its attitude toward the outside world, including foreign markets and firms.

An Imperial (But Not Imperialist) Heritage

To understand China's aspirations in the twenty-first century, we need to go back more than two millennia to an Imperial system that, despite periodic breakdowns, lasted into the daybreak of the twentieth century. This period oversaw China's greatest achievements, its rise to a major regional power that, over extended time periods, was probably the most advanced world civilization. The Imperial system was underpinned by a quasi-religious philosophy, whose founder, Confucius, lived hundreds of years earlier, and who had the benefit of thousands of years of Chinese civilization before him. Confucianism, eventually becoming the state orthodoxy, was but one piece in a surprisingly diverse ideological scene, which included, among other philosophies and religions, Taoism, Buddhism Legalism, and Mohism. Confucianism split into diverse schools of thoughts, which often incorporated elements from the other bases, providing a rich mix that enabled Chinese rulers to anchor their actions in the ideological bases that suited them best.

Confucius upheld scholarship as the most important human activity. It was surpassed only by bureaucratic service, which enabled the scholar to "bring his merits to account," a caveat mostly absent in Western thought. Decades of Communist rule notwithstanding, Confucian elements such as discipline, stability, scholarly achievement, and the prestige of the officialdom have survived into the modern era. Other Confucian principles, such as disdain for military and economic activity, are downplayed today because they challenge current ambitions, reinforcing the regime's tendency to mold culture and ideology to fit national and Party objectives. China retained the importance of ideological legitimacy well into the reform period.

Within the court, and often in the upper echelons of the bureaucracy, Legalism served as the guiding light. This philosophy, which underwrote China's unification under the Qin dynasty, prescribed a codified and ruthlessly enforced system of rules and obligations (rather than rights). The family unit was leveraged as a mechanism of control, establishing a system of mutual responsibility that would later be resuscitated by the Communist regime. Chairman Mao, who was as familiar with China's ideological past as with Marxism-Leninism, favored Mohism, a philosophy that placed the nation above all else and had little use for individual needs or aspirations.

The Imperial Bureaucracy

Confucian teachings, combined with Legalist practices, served as the basis for the Imperial bureaucracy, which, during the two millennia of its existence (intermittently broken by internal infighting and disintegration), developed and implemented organizational and operational principles that would survive in one form or another for thousands of years (and eventually implemented in what is ironically viewed today as a Western model of administration). Among those principles was the world's first merit-based examination system, which was later the model for a modern civil service in Europe. The examination system opened doors to qualified applicants of almost any social rank, allowing them to obtain positions of power and enormous prestige within a professional bureaucracy. (Historical depictions of the Great Constellation showed a citizen pleading before a bureaucrat.) This bureaucracy consisted of a sophisticated system of multiple ministries operating at the central, provincial, and county levels. It not only managed the nation but also provided checks and balances, constraining the power of the Imperial court.

The professional bureaucracy enabled the Chinese ruler to maintain control over vast tracts of land that lacked in transportation and communications. At its height, typically during the early years of the dynastic cycle, the bureaucracy lived up to its lofty principles of universal merit. When things started to go astray, the administration plagued by greed and corruption, it was usually a signal that the dynastic cycle had begun to turn, a decline had set and would end with the eventual demise of the dynasty. On the ground, the most important person in the system was the district magistrate, who exercised unlimited control over its district. A product of the examination system, the district magistrate was a broad generalist and a man of letters, who was assisted by a group of professional experts in finance, public works, and the like that he personally recruited. The magistrate was not only the supreme administrative authority in his jurisdiction; he was also the judge, the policeman, and the warden. Indeed, the concept of separation of powers was—and to a large extent remains—alien to China, which partially explains why the country still does not have an independent judiciary. Today, judicial decisions are still made by bureaucrats, a vast number of whom lack even rudimentary legal training and whose decisions can be overturned by other bureaucrats. This explains why foreign companies can rarely get a fair hearing in a Chinese court, not to mention enforcement of a favorable ruling if one were to come.

Despite its shortcomings, the Imperial bureaucracy was the most formidable administrative apparatus of its time. Crucially, it relied on cooperation from local, lineage-based leadership to control a vast, diverse, and often hard to access territory. In an arrangement that would last well into the modern period, the local leadership was entrusted with power and autonomy, with a surprisingly small number of central bureaucrats intervening only in issues judged to be of the utmost importance. Together with the autonomy exercised by the local officialdom, this created an environment where local interests would flourish and where regions would repeatedly flaunt attempts by the center to centralize and solidify its rule. This has been the origin of the well-worn expression "the sky is high and the emperor is far away," still in use today in independent-minded areas.

While it did not encourage originality or create an infrastructure to support innovations, the Imperial period saw the development of inventions, such as paper and gunpowder, which changed the course of human civilization. Where China lacked was in developing the mindset and structure with which to establish generalized principles of science, which resulted in the country lacking a sustainable innovation stream. China also lacked the ability to diffuse and apply innovation in its economy and military, a shortcoming that has come to head when the army failed to forestall the invading Mongols and Manchu; it found itself in the same predicament centuries later when it encountered the West. What the bureaucratic system was good at was maintaining stability and order—in other words, a status quo—which have become liabilities when the pace of technological change has accelerated. The lesson was not lost on the modern leadership, who saw the advancement of China's scientific capabilities as key not only to economic reform but also to the nation's ability to reclaim its geo-political status.

China and Its Neighbors

Like the Roman Empire in the western hemisphere, the influence of Imperial China on surrounding nations—particularly Korea and Japan but also further afield—was enormous. The culture, writing system, government institutions, and many other vital elements of the civilizations of neighboring countries owe much of their beginning to China, arriving by way of direct or indirect contact. (For instance, much of China's influence on Japan came via Korea.) This diffusion of Chinese knowledge and institutions was not achieved by force or the threat of force. In sharp contrast to Rome and other regional powers of the time that expanded their domain by military means and proceeded to force their system of government and culture upon the conquered, China's neighbors voluntarily adopted what they viewed as advanced elements of culture and government. This pattern of diffusion corresponded to the Chinese view that saw no need to force its system on others. After all, China was "the Middle Kingdom" (the literal translation of its Chinese name), the most civilized, cultured, and advanced nation on earth. It was up to the people living outside China (labeled "barbarians," or "semi-barbarians" if living at a closer perimeter and paying tribute to the Chinese emperor) to adopt its civilized ways. Even when occupied by foreign dynasties (first the Mongols and then the Manchu), China's advanced civilization, combined with its sheer size, ensured that the foreign conquerors adopted Chinese ways rather than the other way around.

The Imperial Imprint

China's Imperial history continues to play an important role in its view of the world. The current official line on the period is still critical of the "feudal" past, but there is no mistake about the pride in the Imperial legacy. China sees itself as one of—if not the longest—surviving world civilizations, and the regime—if not the entire populace—is keenly aware of the country's historical roots. Like the Imperial dynasties before it, the current Chinese leadership is ever mindful of identifying historical precedents, parallels, and justifications for its current actions. When preparing to launch its first manned space flight, Chinese media recalled the legend of a Chinese bureaucrat who purportedly blew himself into space centuries ago using multiple rockets attached to his official chair.

China's Imperial past projects a strong shadow on the country today. First, it sets an extremely high level of ambition. The bar is set at restoring the country's position as a—if not *the*—leading civilization, one that is envied and emulated by other nations. Overtaking once-follower Japan and, to a lesser extent, Korea remains a key success benchmark for now, but in the long range, the aspiration is to become a world leader and not merely a regional leader. A second legacy of China's Imperial past is the tradition of bureaucratically controlled economic activity. This seems to stand in contrast to the current effort to free and liberalize the economy, but it establishes the principle that national interests precede economic rules, a principle that fits well, for instance, with the idea of supporting "strategic" or "pillar" industries. The tradition of bureaucratic rule also implies no separation of powers, with the judicial and the legislative being in essence instruments of the executive branch. (In modern China, all three branches are under the rule of the Party.)

A third imprint of China's Imperial past is the persistence of local interests that compete for power with each other and especially with the center. This implies the continuation of local fiefdoms that make their own rules and defend their own interests even when in conflict with Beijing. For instance, while the central leadership has designated three or four players to become its future "GM, Ford, and Chrysler," local authorities defiantly protect their hundred plus automotive protégés, holding for a better deal in the eventual consolidation process. A fourth impact of China's Imperial past is an ambivalence toward corruption, which is permitted yet periodically curbed when viewed as "overdone" to the point of signaling "dynastic decline." A fifth imprint is the importance of ideological and historical legitimacy. During the Nationalist period, the Confucian analects were replaced by Sun Yat-sen's Three Principles of the People. When the Communists came to power, it was the turn of Marxism-Leninism-Mao Zedong's thought; and when the reforms came, it was the writings of Deng Xiaoping. The halfhearted attempts to market the writings of latter leaders signal not only the decline of charismatic leadership but also an unprecedented ideological vacuum. A final lesson of the Imperial period was that success in breeding innovation was of limited value unless combined with the ability to sustain and apply it in the real world. Bureaucracy and technology had to somehow meet, even if it meant a deviation from the golden age of years past.

The Modern Era: China and the Foreign Powers

China's view of its more recent history during the nineteenth and early twentieth centuries is one of conflict and strife—both external and internal—and, most of all, humiliation. To China, the West represented the first-ever model of culture, society, and economy that presented an alternative to Chinese ideas and, by virtue of its technological and military prowess, one that threatened the very logic and perceived superiority of the Chinese model. Translated into military power, the overwhelming technological superiority of the West had become painfully clear, and the Chinese also discovered that unlike the Mongols and the Manchu before them, Western powers had no intention of settling into Chinese ways and being "peacefully absorbed." That realization made the initial rejection of Western principles unsustainable and presented China with agonizing alternatives: imitate the West and risk losing its identity, or become its weak protectorate. A third and more appealing option was to find ways to adopt Western technology minus Western values, a recurring theme among successive Chinese social movements and regimes from the late Imperial era through the Republican (1911–1949) and into the Communist period.

The humiliation of China via unequal treaties and foreign powers obtaining extraterritorial rights on Chinese soil did not end with the fall of the empire and the adoption of Western technologies and practices by the newly established Republican regime. China was humiliated again in the 1930s and 1940s by the incursion of Japan, which included the seizure of Chinese territory and the founding of a puppet regime in Manchuria, symbolically headed by China's child emperor. That Japan, an Asian nation who once adopted many Chinese ways now surpassed China by combining Western technology with Japanese fervor, provided yet another reminder that China was hopelessly behind in its quest for stature in a new world.

The Shadow of Humiliation

The period of foreign humiliation taught China a number of lessons that are still in force today. First, the period created strong suspicion regarding the motivations and intentions of foreign nations and the foreign multinationals that were the instrument of foreign domination and for a time even exercised consular powers. Years later, China would reluctantly turn to foreign firms, but this time to extract skills and knowledge. Indeed, the second lesson from the humiliation period was to make sure that China did not become dependent on others, and that technology was a key ingredient of independence. The realization was translated into an emphasis on technology transfer by all means possible—be they special investment incentives or repatriation of foreign-trained talent—to achieve the scope and depth to permit the development of independent research and technology capabilities.

A third imprint of the foreign humiliation period was the forging of a close link between technology and national security, a sector that in China is broadly defined, among other reasons due to the existence of a vast network of firms owned by or having a close relationship to the defense establishment. While the technology-security connection eroded during Mao's heydays on the belief that sheer human power was sufficient to overwhelm any enemy, much of China's advanced technology effort, such as its space enterprise, is conducted within military frameworks. A final takeaway from the period is a quest for combining foreign technology with Chinese—not foreign—values. The correlation assumed by Westerners between free market economics, democracy, and scientific progress is inconsistent with the views of the Chinese leadership (who obviously has a vested interest in the continuation of the present order) but also with those of some other powerful segments, including many of the newly rich for whom the existing system may represent the best of both worlds: capitalist wealth united with Communist protection and subsidies.

China Under Communism

During its first three decades, the People's Republic had a centrally planned system in the Communist tradition, although not nearly as rigid as that of the Soviet Union. The system fluctuated, often dramatically. The first period, 1949 to 1955–56, was one of reconstruction and transition. Expert officialdom in such realms as finance and logistics was retained from the Republican era in the same way that the Republicans retained Imperial officials when they came to power, providing a measure of continuity. Foreign firms continued to operate, but their operations were disrupted and curbed. The second period, the so-called One Man Management, lasted from 1955-6 to 1958-9. It was a replica of the rigid Soviet model, accompanied by the importation of Soviet technology and Soviet thinking and imputed via the education of many Chinese (including some in the current leadership) in the Soviet Union. When the Soviets pulled out, the Chinese soon found out that they could operate the machinery but lacked the capabilities to improve upon the technology beyond limited improvisations. The third period was the Great Leap Forward of 1958–1960, which Chinese later called the Great Leap *Backward*. A disastrous celebration of Maoist ideology, production was pushed to the countryside with horrendous consequences, including mass starvation. Disaster struck again in the form of the Cultural Revolution in 1966, when Mao unleashed his Red Guards on intellectuals and senior officials, dissolving the educational system and much of the organized economy. The campaign lasted until 1968, but its consequences lingered until 1975 and continued to haunt China for decades to come. The Chinese later lamented this time as "the lost decade," the consequences of which are still apparent today in a generation of managers and employees who lack proper education and who are fearful of taking risks lest the ideological wind shift direction again.

The Communist Imprint

The first 30 years of Communist rule taught China a number of valuable lessons. The first lesson was that the combination of ideology and economy was explosive. This created a problem given the importance of ideological legitimacy in Chinese tradition, but China found a way to deal with the challenge. A second lesson was that technology, in its codified, narrow definition, could not deliver more than routine, ongoing performance, and sustained progress required fundamental mental transformation and reorganization of the production system. While it was clear that for reasons of control and political power, the bureaucracy was there to stay (although, as in Imperial times, much of the actual power was vested at the local level), it became evident that it needed to be distanced from technological and economic activities if the country were to progress. A third takeaway from the period was that agglomeration, in the sense of concentrating infrastructure and expertise in selected locations, was necessary even if politically and ideologically suspect. (Mao insisted on replicating operations in multiple provinces, among other reasons because he feared a Soviet attack.) A final and no less important lesson was that the fortunes of the regime were intricately intertwined with those of the nation and, in particular, its economic prosperity. Like their Imperial predecessors, the Communist rulers did not need to be concerned with an election defeat, but rather with the unrest and rebellion that economic hardship could bring about. The fall of the Soviet Union decades later would drive home the risk of a political meltdown underpinned by economic underperformance, a reminder that the "Mandate of Heaven" principle espoused by Confucius' student Mencius was still applicable. (The principle, which was revolutionary at the time, implied that if the emperor failed to deliver prosperity, the citizenry had not only the right but also the duty to unseat him.)

The Reform Period

China officially embarked on the road to reform in October 1978, going through various phases and following a trial-and-error learning curve. Over the next 25 years, the country shifted its investment focus from tourism to light manufacturing, from a policy of forcing foreign investors to take on a Chinese partner to one that permits wholly owned foreign subsidiaries, and from a "catch up" phase to one aimed at achieving global parity. Political struggle continued, with the Tiananmen massacre a reminder that even the reformists in the leadership were not about to relinquish party control, and that democracy, which in the Western mind was associated with economic progress, was not coming any time soon.

The seriousness of the reform effort was such that the leadership was now ready to give up on some of its traditional ways as long as it could achieve a measure of Imperial success—economic prosperity under an unquestioned regime. Determined to achieve genuine technology transfer, the regime was ready to have knowledge—once closely guarded—disseminated to employees, suppliers, consumers, and other constituencies (such as students). It was suspected that technology meant more than blueprints, although the lesson was not brought home until it was revealed that the wholesale importation of production lines from the West did not do enough to improve competitiveness. China needed to build an infrastructure—human, educational, and organizational—to support complex production and build its capabilities, and it was ready to push aside ideology in the process. One of the key statements of China's reform architect Deng Xiaoping was that it did not matter what the color of the cat was, as long as it was able to catch mice. Pretenses regarding the cat's color still counted, however. The Chinese, one senior official of the time confided, were ready to try anything, but would label whatever worked as "socialism."

Lofty Aspirations

Grounded in past glory and modern humiliation, China's aspirations are not merely rapid modernization and joining the ranks of developed nations—it wants no less than to restore its ancient Imperial glory, a small but pertinent symbol of which has been recent purchases by newly affluent Chinese of Chinese arts looted by the West.[1] Restoration means not only a reinstatement of the global economic leadership of bygone centuries (see Exhibit 2-1), but also reestablishment of the nation's stature in politics, culture, and security. If the Chinese Empire was a regional player, today's China sees itself as a global player with interests reaching far beyond its ancient sphere of influence of East Asia. The sentiment is shared by Chinese firms, which may still be focused on their burgeoning domestic market and their immediate surroundings but have their eyes firmly set on global markets. Like Japan before it, increasing domestic competition in various market segments is preparing Chinese firms to face the vagaries of the international marketplace.

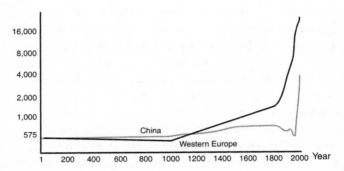

Source: Figure 1 (p. 42): GDP per capita: China and Western Europe: 1–1998 A.D. in Maddison, Angus (2001),
The World Economy: A Millennial Perspective OECD. Copyright, OECD 2001.

Exhibit 2-1   GDP per Capita (in 2002 Dollars): China and Western Europe: 1-1998 A.D.

National Symbols

Like other nondemocratic regimes, China is obsessed with symbols of grandeur. From building the world's tallest building to hosting the Olympics, which is a traditional coming-of-age for Asian nations, symbols are important to the Chinese regime, whose legitimacy increasingly rests on delivering economic performance and growth on the one hand and on nationalist sentiments on the other. Showcase projects are there to impress citizens and outsiders with the regime's capabilities and signal that the aspiration to be counted among the world's leading nations is attainable. Money, when showcase projects are on the line, is no object. Nowhere is the Chinese aspiration more apparent than in its space project. Having launched a satellite in the late 1970s, China has entered the exclusive club of nations launching manned spaced flights, something only the United States and the Soviet Union have achieved. The country's space effort is handled by the military, illustrating the tight connection between national security and technological progress. Truly, space has similar links to national security in the United States and Russia. However, in the U.S., a civilian agency (NASA) is in charge and reserves certain payloads for the military, while in China, the military is in charge of the entire process. Although the scientific value of manned space flights remains debatable, the Chinese leadership cherishes their symbolic value and does not need to deal with the open, public debate that questions their value in the United States.

At this time, China's space effort is mostly an exercise in copying and replication. Its rocket development effort was nurtured by a Chinese scientist previously with America's Jet Propulsion Laboratory, and the capsule used in the manned flight was a Soviet design. China is, however, determined to claim a spot in space and has outlined an ambitious agenda to include a space station as well as an exploration of Mars and other planets. The effort is expected to generate spillovers first to the military but in time to civilian players as well.

Political Aspirations

The political aspirations of (post-World War II) Japan and South Korea have been limited by size, geo-politics, and constitutional constraints. China is not bound by those. It has the largest (although much in need of modernization) standing army in the world, rapidly rising economic muscle, and an emerging standing as a political force to be reckoned with. The country's self-identity encompasses the People's Republic as the nucleus and center of a Greater China that includes Hong Kong (a Chinese Special Administrative Region since 1997) and Taiwan, viewed as a renegade province that should rejoin the mainland under a "One Country Two Systems" arrangement of the sort applied to Hong Kong, or, if necessary, by force. China also maintains a special relationship with multiracial but predominantly Chinese Singapore, as well as with the overseas Chinese community whom it sees as a key ingredient in China's progress. Economically speaking, the vision of a Greater China is already a reality. The economies of Hong Kong and Taiwan are closely integrated with the mainland economy in which they and the overseas Chinese are major investors.

The concept of Greater China fits well with the country's political vision of a future world power, one that will ultimately replace the Soviet Union as a counterbalance to American power. This vision received a boost after September 11 when China became a pivotal player in a world threatened by radical elements. While China has restive Muslim minorities in its western provinces, it is strongly suspicious of radicalism and religious movements, which, together with its control structure, make it an indispensable and reliable partner in the war on terrorism. The country is increasingly assertive in world affairs, although its influence still rests more within the Asian sphere. China's mediation between the United States and North Korea allows it to showcase its ability and willingness to leverage its relationship with multiple players (the U.S., North Korea, South Korea, Russia) to achieve stability, a goal it holds dearly both at home and abroad. Still to come in the not-so-distant future is a China more involved with international institutions, such as the United Nations and the World Trade Organization (WTO), and one that will leverage its increasing political and economic muscle to yield influence via foreign aid, military assistance, and the like, just like the United States, the former Soviet Union, and the European Union (EU).

Internally, the political agenda of the Chinese leadership does not include transition to democracy. China has already defied western assumptions regarding the essential correlation between a democratic system and economic progress, and it's likely to continue to do so. While the political system may be relaxed in the future, it is more likely to include local self-leadership of the sort exercised during Imperial times and possibly elections at that level; or it may transform into a Singapore-type democracy where open elections are held but the winner can be declared before exit poles are announced. Side by side with continuous liberalization, the Chinese state and its bureaucratic apparatus will continue to yield enormous power in guiding the direction of the Chinese economy. That this seems a contradiction to the Western observer should serve as yet one more reminder that China is—and is likely to remain—different.

Economic Aspirations

China's economic aspirations are aligned strongly with its political ambitions, and the regime is aware more than most of the close connection between the two. China sees itself as a rising economic power, and is determined to overcome any remaining obstacles to reaching that goal, be it a reform of its financial system or accelerated privatization of the state sector. Since the start of reforms in 1978, China has taken a cautious and incremental course designed not only to maintain stability but also to achieve sustainable transformation of macro economic, enterprise, and individual players. A comparison with Russia and its ill-advised (by Western economists) "shock therapy" seems to vindicate China's decision to seek incremental change; it also reiterates China's determination to chart an independent course rather than blindly imitate Western models. Extrapolating from the experience of other countries in forecasting China's future course is a risky exercise.

Ever mindful of the human element, a senior Chinese official prophetically told me in the 1980s that the Chinese economic revolution would be completed when a new generation of managers is at the helm. Twenty-five years have passed, and with a generation commonly measured in 30-year terms, the prediction is on the mark. It was only in the mid 1990s that China came up with a bankruptcy law and only in late 2003 that the leadership decided to confer the rights granted to state-owned enterprises to the private sector, equalizing the playing field. China will soon be ready to move to the next phase that will take it to the next level, from subcontracting to development and design and further to branded production. At home, Chinese firms have become formidable competitors to foreign multinationals, and the best of this crop is ready to move into global markets. Winners will not only be market- selected but will be judged by the political leadership on their perceived contribution to national interests, party loyalty, and other nonmarket factors that will reflect the penchant and need for continuous control. They will increasingly come from knowledge-intensive industries, especially those that are considered "strategic"—that is, having national security applications and producing key inputs for other sectors, such as electronic chips. A special preference will be accorded to those highest on the knowledge chain: research and development entities that produce knowledge.

In the meantime, China's service sector remains underdeveloped, among other reasons because it is only now beginning to open up to foreign competition. It, too, however, has a place in the nation's vision. While firmly committed to manufacturing, the leadership understands that sectors of the service economy, such as consulting, are knowledge intensive, while others are essential to the development of manufacturing. Without capabilities in finance, logistic services, and the like, Chinese firms are unlikely to become successful multinationals. Further, development in transportation and communications is essential for the internal development of the Chinese economy as well as for the incorporation of the country into the global economy. No less important, the service economy, in particular financial services, is key to the maintenance of social and political stability. With a "safety net" of social security in its infancy, a solid financial and insurance network is vital for the country's future development.

After a millennia-long roller coaster ride from glory to rags, the Middle Kingdom is on the ascent again, determined to capture not only the splendor of the past, but also the promise of the future. China's leadership will make every conceivable effort not to lose its "Mandate of Heaven" this time around.

3

Like No Other

China is not the first economy to rise rapidly from the ranks of developing countries or to emerge from the ashes of war and internal strife to become an industrial power. In the aftermath of World War II, Japan and Germany (with the help of a large infusion of U.S. assistance) revived industries ravaged by defeat and destruction and managed to turn them into "miracle economies." South Korea, Hong Kong, Taiwan, and Singapore emerged from Japanese occupation to become "tigers" or "little dragons" with high-growth economies and rapidly rising living standards. Taiwan managed to accommodate a major influx of mainlanders in 1949, while South Korea withstood war and insurgency to transform from an agrarian society into an industrial powerhouse. Both enjoyed generous U.S. help but were able to translate it into lasting progress. Thailand, Malaysia, Indonesia, the Philippines, and Vietnam were alternately hailed as "new generation tigers" destined to follow in the footsteps of South Korea, Taiwan, Singapore, and Hong Kong, although the Asian financial crisis and internal upheaval undermined their progress. Most recently, India has launched its first serious economic reforms and is now competing for the multinational investment it ejected in the 1970s.

Is there anything special about China, then? Is the country just one more link in this long chain of developing economies on their way up, receiving the baton from the little dragons only to pass it quickly onto the hand of the new kid on the block—Vietnam or perhaps India? And will China end up as a "paper tiger," its imprint seemingly fizzling like that of a stagnating Japan or the little dragons following the Asian crisis? The question is not merely academic: If China is nothing more than another emerging economy on its way up, then its impact should be temporary, confined and, above all, predictable in form and path. This, in turn, will make it easy to draw lessons from the impact of China's predecessors, assess its competitiveness vis-à-vis its current counterparts, and above all, devise strategies and techniques to deal with the challenge.

The argument made in this book is that the rise of China in the early part of the twenty-first century is distinctive and has more in common with the rise of the United States in the twentieth century than with the advance of its Asian neighbors; the repercussions of its climb are equally monumental. The uniqueness of the Chinese ascent is rooted not only in China's enormous population base; after all, India also has passed the one billion mark. It's also not rooted in China's huge economy (Japan is still the world's number two economy in nominal dollars) or even its rapid growth (Japan and the four little dragons each enjoyed a higher growth rate at some point), although the combination of these factors is special to China. China's exceptionality is about a special legacy, different institutions, sky-high aspirations, and a one-of-a-kind combination of resources, capabilities, and bargaining power. China's uniqueness is also about timing. It is ascending during a dramatic acceleration in globalization, the emergence of powerful multilateral institutions such as the World Trade Organization (WTO), the most significant geopolitical realignment since the fall of the Soviet Union, and increasing pressures associated with economic restructuring in major industrialized nations, especially the United States. This constellation of interdependent events has no direct precedent; it is also unlikely to be replicated elsewhere any time soon. It will force nations, firms, and individuals to question accepted assumptions, reject past analogies, and develop strategic responses that do not currently exist in their repertoire.

Consider this: China is the only Communist nation (admittedly with an increasingly open economy) to achieve rapid economic real growth over a sustainable time period. It's the only emerging economy with an authoritarian regime that seeks, but finds it increasingly difficult, to maintain tight control on individual freedoms and expression even as it frees ever-larger segments of economic activity. China is the only developing country that yearly pulls in an amount of foreign investment greater than that of all other developing economies combined, and that now attracts more international investment dollars than any other market, developed or developing.[1] China also receives technology transfer at a pace, scope, and depth never before seen in a developing country, especially one that is not considered a close ally of its benefactors. And, among all emerging economies in the past 50 years, China is by far the most ambitious in its goals and the most determined to fulfill them.

Understanding the experience of China's predecessors and counterparts at home and in international markets and assessing the efficacy of the responses it generated is important not only in judging China's uniqueness. The comparison is also vital for our ability to identify the benchmarks set by the Chinese government and the models and strategies it pursues in its continued development effort at home and in its expansion into foreign markets. This, in turn, will enable us to better grasp China's future impact on the rest of the world.

Is China a New Japan?

No other country comes up so often in discussions of the U.S.-China trade relationship as Japan. It is easy to see why: Both China and Japan are Asian nations that at one point were considered a national security threat to the United States (a familiar American sentiment about Japan in the early 1980s was that it won the military war with Japan but lost the subsequent economic battle), a suspicion that lingered even as geopolitical realignment brought them closer to American interests. Both countries at one time were the number-one contributor to the American trade deficit, manipulated exchange rates to enhance competitiveness, flaunted intellectual property rights (albeit China on a much grander scale), and erected a litany of trade barriers restricting the importation of American goods. Both were accused of taking a free ride on U.S. open markets without opening their own. The similarities end there, however, as does the usefulness of the analogy. But first, some background.

In the 1970s, the U.S. media started carrying a growing number of stories: first on Japanese imports, and later on Japanese investments in the United States. Japanese complaints about being singled out (when was the last time you have read an article on British investments in America?) fell on deaf ears. Books describing the Japanese threat proliferated on bookstore shelves, just as utopian accounts of Japanese management were hitting the top of the best-sellers lists. High-profile purchases such as the Rockefeller Center, famous golf courses, and high-end Hawaiian hotels produced even more alarming accounts of a rising power that was bent on taking over the American economy. It did not help that many Japanese also bought into the belief that theirs was a system superior to any other. In the mind of many Americans and Japanese, the rise of Japan was inevitably linked to a decline of American civilization.

Nowhere was the Japanese threat more visible and threatening than in this most conspicuous symbol of the American economic might and way of life: the automobile. Japan, which designated automotive as a strategic industry already in the 1950s, restarted its car industry after the war by reverse engineering American models and taking advantage of orders from the American military in Korea. Less than two decades later, Japanese makers were already shipping product to the U.S.—first a few thousands units annually and, by the early 1970s, hundreds of thousands of cars per year. During all those years, U.S. car exports to Japan remained at the same dismal level of a few thousand cars annually. Japan's initial success in exporting cars to America was first attributed in the public's mind to the oil crisis of October 1973 (in reality, the crisis merely accelerated an export surge that was already in full swing), which enabled many to argue that the Japanese were merely lucky—they happened to have economy cars for sale just when the market needed them. When Japanese manufacturers extended their gains, another, not unfounded argument came about: Japan was not playing fair, artificially lowering the value of the yen to boost exports while erecting barriers to American exports. The same criticism was directed decades later toward China.

In the late 1970s and early 1980s, another explanation for Japan's success gained ground: perhaps Japan was simply producing higher-quality products at a more reasonable price, and to improve competitiveness, American firms needed to learn from Japan in such realms as quality control, productivity, and human resource management. The honeymoon with "Japanese management" was about to begin. U.S. business schools that until then did not want anything to do with Japan or any other Asian country began a period of enchantment with everything Japanese. Centers for Japanese business were established complete with teahouses and endowed positions, and Japan became a favorite topic of academic research. Scholars soon discovered that Japan had a tendency to defy Western thinking on such key issues as the relationship between exchange rates and trade, or, in the words of some economists of the time, that "Japan did not fit the model."

Analogies of Response

It is hard to imagine that only 20 years ago Detroit auto workers publicly hacked a Toyota to show their disgust with Japanese imports, when today Toyota is becoming the third largest U.S. car maker, displacing Chrysler (now owned by Germany's Daimler), whose near death triggered much of the alarm about Japanese competition in the first place. Yet, it would be wrong to believe that the experience did not leave its marks on the American psyche and on the strategic repertoire of U.S. firms, the federal government, industrial unions, and other significant constituencies who are now drawing analogies from the Japanese experience to China. As misplaced as some of these analogies may be, they cast a long shadow over the interpretation of China's advance and the efficacy of the reaction to the challenge.

One supposed lesson from the Japanese challenge is that it has been exaggerated. After all, once-feared Japan later entered a prolonged period of painful economic stagnation and was forced to unload many of its more visible U.S. investments, often suffering big losses. The sale of the Japanese-owned Rockefeller Center back to U.S. interests just as the New York market was about to take off again reaffirmed the belief of many Americans that business acumen was on their side and there was no reason to worry about competition from Japan or any other country. The analogy implies that the Chinese threat is also overplayed, and the trade imbalances and dislocations it would bring are by nature temporary and would be resolved by market forces, if not by the rapid transformation of the U.S. into a service-based economy. This remains the prevalent view among economic observers.

If the feeling that Japan's threat was exaggerated took hold, it does not sit well with the facts. The U.S. trade imbalance with Japan that ballooned in the 1970s and 1980s may have stabilized in the 1990s but remains over $60 billion a year, second only to China's. The big three auto makers (treating Chrysler as a separate entity from its German parent) never recovered the market share they lost to the Japanese and are now fighting to defend their last turf of trucks and SUVs against relentless Japanese inroads often led by Made in the U.S.A. models. Employment in the industry is a fraction of that prior to the Japanese advance (although automation and chronic industry overcapacity have played a central role, too). In the meantime, Japanese consumers continue to frown upon American-made cars even as foreign investment in the Japanese automotive industry has grown substantially.

Vitally, the Japan experience exposes the inefficacy of many of the responses undertaken by American industry and unions to counter foreign competition. After all, the trade deficit with Japan persisted in the face of "voluntary" quotas, dramatic realignment in exchange rates, and continuous U.S. government pressure to pry open Japanese markets. The deficit also survived the establishment of U.S. transplants by the major Japanese manufacturers (together with their suppliers), who were supposed to export back to Japan (but rarely did), and a dramatic restructuring, including marked improvement in quality and productivity, by American makers. In fact, it now seems that the main factor curtailing the Japanese surplus has been the transfer of Japanese manufacturing capacity to China, which by and large shifted a portion of the deficit from one county to the other. Worse, it appears that some of the responses undertaken in the U.S. to fight the deficit with Japan may have backfired. For instance, limiting Japanese car imports in unit amounts as part of the quotas only accelerated their up market shift because this became the only way to augment export revenues. The shift culminated in the establishment of luxury divisions by Honda (Acura), Toyota (Lexus), and Nissan (Infiniti), which targeted the Cadillac and the Lincoln customer, along with German imports. Japanese firms have come full circle from low-cost producers to full-range competitors charging a premium for the perceived quality of their products. The U.S. manufacturing industry, on its part, discovered that the up market was not protected from Asian competition either.

Japan, China, and the Limits of Analogy

Analogies are a useful lens through which to see the world, but as proven time and time again, they have their limitations. To be sure, China and Japan share a number of traits, starting with partial similarity in philosophy, religion, and institutions (such as Confucianism, although the philosophy did not become state orthodoxy in Japan until the late nineteenth century, precisely when the Chinese started to suspect it was detrimental to modernization). Both countries have been an enigma to Western observers, who oscillated between suspicion and an unadulterated admiration for their ancient civilizations and modern achievements. Both nations also have historical baggage: Japan as a member of the Axis during World War II ("remember Pearl Harbor" was often used as a slogan against Japanese imports) and China as a member of the Communist block (targeted by U.S. unions for its human right violations) during much of the cold war. Both Japan and China have had the misfortune of lacking development infrastructure, later reinterpreted as a boon because it enabled them to leapfrog countries with investment sunk in older technologies. Both have benefited from favorable geo-political circumstances: Japan was helped by the cold war, with many Japanese firms getting their first overseas orders from the American military in Korea, and with the U.S. reluctant to pressure a reliable ally in a largely hostile Asia with a Communist China and a Soviet-affiliated India. In the aftermath of September 11, China appears to play a role as a potential ally in the fight against terrorism and in containing North Korea.

Japan ran a coordinated industrial effort that gave priority to "strategic industries" while maintaining competition within each of those industries—something China would imitate later. In their foray into foreign markets, both Japan and China used an artificially weak currency to support exports; in fact, both continue to do so today. Both countries also have used trade barriers to block foreign—especially U.S. imports. Both benefited from a lingering perception that they were unlikely to become viable competitors with the possible exception of cheap, low-technology products. Then and now, this proved to be a serious mistake.

Similarities notwithstanding, China and Japan differ in a number of key areas. One vital difference is size: Although the Japanese economy is larger than that of China's in nominal terms, the allure of a vast and rapidly growing Chinese market with pent-up demand for products and services translates into greater leverage with trade partners than Japan ever had. China's size gives it another advantage: While Japan moved in less than a generation from a low-cost manufacturer to a high-cost producer (and, unlike the U.S., it did not have immigration to cushion the transition), China has a vast, untapped hinterland with a huge supply of workers, which will permit it to move up the technology scale without sacrificing its present cost advantage for years to come. China will thus use its dominance in labor-intensive production to advance the knowledge-intensive industries of the future. In addition to having Hong Kong and Taiwan (and to some extent Singapore) as capital providers and knowledge catalysts, China has a vibrant overseas community that plays a major role in its development and globalization. Japan had none. China has the benefit of much larger foreign investment (which Japan rejected at the time for fear of foreign domination and as a threat to Japanese culture). China is also ready to open up its educational system, something Japan never did, and in addition to sending its students abroad, China is a host to many foreign students from Asia and the West. Plus, while Japan's World War defeat limited its future defense expenditure and deployment, China is a member of the Security Council and is becoming more involved in world affairs, participation it will later leverage for economic advantage.

China's potentially stronger impact is also anchored in the timing of its ascent. Its rise and challenge to its trading nations come at an earlier level of development than Japan's, driven by stronger internal pressures to provide employment (Japanese unemployment was low in the 1970s and 1980s) and relying on a much lower cost base. This means that, with a few exceptions, the Japanese strategy of transferring production to the U.S. is unlikely to be replicated at this time, which limits the prospects for employment absorption by implants. (Japanese auto transplants by and large avoided veterans of the U.S. industry but did hire other Americans.) Another difference between China and Japan is that the United States handled its trade conflicts with Japan on a bilateral basis, while conflicts with China are handled under the multilateral WTO regime. Given China's trade distribution (a huge surplus with the U.S., a moderate surplus with the European Union, and a deficit with Asia), continuous acrimony between the U.S. and the EU, and a rising conflict between developing and developed nations over farm subsidies, it would be difficult for the U.S. to garner support for policies limiting China's entry to its markets, especially since much of the world, according to Transparency International, views the U.S. as an unfair trader.

The Innovation Imperative

A crucial difference between Japan and China has to do with their capacity for innovation and propensity for entrepreneurial and international activities, all crucially important in today's global economy. Innovative capacity is not only a function of the number of scientists and engineers (although China is doing well on that measure as well), but is also a product of legacy factors. Historically, China has been an innovator, and Japan has been an imitator or an incremental improver, rarely producing radical innovations. The Japanese have often been critical of their education system as promoting rote learning and group conformity while stifling innovation. The Chinese education system suffered from some of the same ills, but not during its entire history. During many periods of its Imperial past, Chinese cities were host to residents of foreign nationality, religion, and culture. Now, with the help of foreign investors (never fully welcome in Japan), Chinese are building on that tradition.

Entrepreneurial activity has been limited in Japan, a result not only of lack of education for innovation, but also of low tolerance for uncertainty and prestige factors (the best graduates of Japan's universities sought government service or corporate employment), a nepotistic production and distribution network that kept outsiders at bay, and a lack of supporting infrastructure (such as venture capital firms). China, despite its legacy of bureaucratic control, tolerated entrepreneurial activity for much of its history. During Imperial times, some Chinese merchants accumulated vast sums of money, although the money often went into preparation for or the purchase of bureaucratic positions rather than to further economic activity. Some entrepreneurial activity survived into the mid 1950s and was gradually renewed from 1979 onward, which means that, unlike the Soviet Union, the reforming Chinese have had experienced entrepreneurs in their ranks. Finally, the overseas Chinese brought with them an enormous level of entrepreneurial ability and enthusiasm. As minorities barred from government and agricultural employment in their adopted countries, Chinese have founded flourishing businesses that have later invested in the "motherland." In contrast, the largest group of Japanese descendents outside the U.S., in Brazil, has been more a source of menial labor for a society fearful of heterogeneity than a provider of investment, knowledge, and global contacts.

The Chinese advantage in innovation, size, and timing suggests that as substantial as the Japanese impact has been, the Chinese impact is likely to be much bigger, more sustainable, and broader in terms of economic sectors. The initial impact will not be cushioned this time by foreign investment inflows to partially offset job losses, or by exchange rate realignment. Such alignment, as the Japan experience shows, will not make much of a difference anyway, and even less so in China where the government maintains a tighter grip and can met subsidies and other incentives as a way to compensate for exchange rate adjustment. Likewise, erecting barriers in the form of quotas may backfire by accelerating China's push into higher margin domains.

Dragons, Large and Small

In the 1980s and 1990s, Japan slowly faded from U.S. media screens. Its foreign investment fell from a hiatus funded by low real interest rates, easy bank financing, and an asset price bubble. With the bursting of the Tokyo stock market in the late 1980s, Japanese firms had their bank loans recalled and unloaded U.S. assets often at fire sale prices. This signaled to Americans that the coast was clear: The Japanese threat had receded, its economy beginning a long period of stagnation. The American model had been vindicated again—or so it seemed. While growth and job creation resumed, the United States did not return to balanced trade in the twentieth century.

As Japan vanished from the American psyche, the void was filled by a second wave of Asian imports. The four "tigers" or "little dragons"— Taiwan, Hong Kong, South Korea, and Singapore—were initially regarded as "new Japans." Indeed, while these four territories resented Japan for its brutal colonial and wartime record, they viewed it a model of Asian success worthy of emulation. Taking a page from Japan, these economies started by aggressively pursuing the labor-intensive, low-technology areas that Japan, with its higher cost structure, was forced to desert, but later turned up-market as a reaction to rising costs and Chinese competition. Today, the "tigers" are closely linked with the

Greater China economy as investors and partners, and they are major contributors to the growth of intra-Asian trade. As a group, but also separately, the tigers remain major models that China closely follows as it charts its own course.

Hong Kong

A British colony for a century and a half, Hong Kong served as the gateway to China for much of that time. In the 1960s and 1970s, Hong Kong was a thriving manufacturing base producing low cost goods, most of which did not compete directly with a Japan that was already climbing the technological ladder. Always reliant on its physical proximity but superior governance to China, Hong Kong has become more closely dependent on the mainland after the launch of the reforms, a closeness cemented in 1984 with the signing of the Joint Declaration, returning Hong Kong to Chinese rule in 1997. Feeling the heat from other tigers, as well as from newly industrialized bases in Malaysia and Indonesia and competition for its textile exports from lower cost bases, Hong Kong firms seized on the proximity and ethnic relations and shifted manufacturing operations to the Chinese mainland, initially in the adjacent South and later across China. This enabled the territory to develop a competitive advantage as an entrepreneurial and managerial junction rather than a manufacturing base. Today, there are many toy producers in Hong Kong, but not a single toy factory remains. The territory, competing with the mainland's urban centers (in particular Shanghai), is trying to reinvent itself as a financial and service center, a revealing challenge for those who see the future of the United States as a service hub.

At first sight, Hong Kong's experience bears little relevance to China. Small in size, "Westernized" on the surface, and a free market, Hong Kong does not cause the feeling of concern in the West that Japan or mainland China have elicited. However, Hong Kong has demonstrated important qualities that have been infused to the mainland and are becoming indigenous to it. These include experience in climbing the technological ladder (admittedly up to a point) via massive investment in higher education, a record of retaining knowledge capabilities while shifting production to cheaper locations, a strong entrepreneurial spirit, and the capability to develop and run not only small business, but also large, diversified global conglomerates, such as Hutchison Whampoa.

With the blessing and support of the mainland authorities, Hong Kong has also shown that with massive reserves and steadfast determination, it is possible to defend an exchange rate peg in the face of ferocious attacks by speculators, who have managed to bring down such pegs in other countries. This does not bode well for American hopes to strengthen the yuan even if it were to be floated.

Taiwan

Following the defeat of the Nationalists in the Chinese civil war, Chiang Kai-shek's forces retreated to the island of Taiwan where, with American help, they established a manufacturing-based economy consisting of mostly small, family-owned firms as well as some large state-owned large industrial enterprises. Like the mainland, Taiwan also started its foray into the global economy as a low-cost manufacturer but eventually moved up-market, sustaining labor-intensive activities by relocating to the mainland. It gradually developed technological capabilities that were rarely cutting edge but still provided advanced, specialized, niche capabilities and "value for money," permitting the emergence of technology conglomerates such as Acer. Taiwan also successfully used agglomeration, which is now taken for granted by scholars and practitioners alike as an effective strategy for growing technical capabilities, co-locating multiple competitors and supporting industries in a successful bid to achieve global leadership in products like notebook computers. Taiwan is also the first ever democracy in a Chinese society—and a vibrant one at that. This example is sometimes cited as a future model for China, although the huge differences in size alter the order and stability equation that the People's Republic of China (PRC) utilizes as a justification for one-party rule; this and other factors suggest that those pinning their hope on China's democratization may be in for a disappointment.

Although Taiwan maintained a large trade surplus with the U.S. for many years, it did not come under much scrutiny. Much of this had to do with geo-politics. Until the formal recognition of the PRC as China's government in the late 1970s, Taiwan was viewed by the U.S. as the legitimate ruler of all of China and a bastion against the spread of Communism. Even after recognition of the PRC, U.S. support for Taiwan continued, and successive U.S. administrations remained fiercely opposed to the Chinese threat to take the island by force. Under those circumstances, the U.S. government was reluctant to pressure Taiwan on trade issues. Another factor that helped Taiwan (as well as Hong Kong and Singapore) avoid scrutiny and blame is that its exports consisted primarily of intermediate inputs incorporated into other products and often sold under other brand names. In contrast, Japan's exports relied heavily on end products, and its largest trade surplus was in the highly visible automotive category. The PRC enjoys similar benefits in areas like automotive components (with a China-made car in the U.S. market still years away), but it is keen on building global Made in China brands.

Singapore

The third (predominantly) Chinese tiger, Singapore, is similar to Hong Kong in its small size, relatively free market, and entrepôt position (more with Southeast Asia). With the exception of occasional flare-ups about media censorship, the U.S. relationship with Singapore has been good, and trade has not been a major issue of contention. Singapore remains a center for high-tech manufacturing as it tries, like Hong Kong, to lure service providers and strengthen its position as a regional headquarters for multinationals. Singapore's relationship with China is close, underpinned by demographics (Singapore is almost 80 percent Chinese) and consummated via extensive foreign investment. In many ways, its economy is complementary to that of China, and the same may be said about its political and social system. Officially a democracy, the likelihood of regime change in Singapore appears to be extremely low, making it a potential model for the mainland in the future. There are other things the mainland regime likes about Singapore: In many ways, it is the ideal Confucian society, with patriarchal leadership, heavy socialization, emphasis on discipline, and overseen by a competent, prestigious, and highly compensated bureaucracy. The island nation even has Confucian academies and is probably as close as you get to a modern-era reincarnation of a Chinese empire ruled by an enlightened dynasty and a merit-based administration.

South Korea

The only non-Chinese member of the tigers (although heavily influenced by Confucianism) is South Korea. Rising from the destruction of a long and abusive Japanese occupation, war, and internal strife, South Korea, whose GDP was similar to that of many African countries in the 1950s, turned itself within a relatively short time from an agrarian economy to an industrial powerhouse, even as it maintained a considerable defense expenditure, a feat that made it an enticing model in the eyes of the Chinese leadership, which remains the increasingly reluctant patron of North Korea.

South Korea's modernization charge was led by the *chaebols*, family-owned conglomerates that, with generous government support, grew to an enormous size and diversified into any imaginable activity. These conglomerates were responsible for the vast majority of Korean exports, with small and medium-size companies playing an important but largely supporting role. This has begun to change following the Asian financial crisis, which required bailout by the International Monetary Fund (IMF) and which exposed many of the vulnerabilities of the chaebol system, such as lack of transparency, weak governance, unchecked borrowing, and lack of strategic focus. Surprisingly, perhaps, China has not lost interest in the chaebols as a model for Chinese conglomerates, although it has certainly taken their weaknesses to heart. The ability of such chaebols as LG and Samsung to restructure and globalize convinced the Chinese leadership that they should continue to provide viable blueprints (albeit perhaps not under family ownership for now), except that China will try to leapfrog into more focused business groups. China also wants to learn from South Korea how to effectively use returning students to beef up its technological and managerial capabilities.

In relation to trade, China has noted the boost Korean exports received from the devaluation of the won during the Asian crisis, and the memory lingers as another reason to resist calls for strengthening the yuan. Another lesson China has drawn from the Korean experience is the importance of penetrating other developing markets—in particular in Asia—as a way of hedging against a trade backlash in the United States and other developed economies, and as part of a strategy to build a strong Asian market to match Europe and the Americas.

The Asian Crisis, Misinterpreted

The Asian financial crisis, starting in Thailand in 1997 and quickly spreading to other Asian nations with a contagion effect of falling stock and asset prices, was a watershed in the region. Asian economies switched almost instantly from having the highest growth rates in the world to negative growth. The title "financial crisis" was somewhat of a misnomer; the crisis was as much about institutional and managerial failure, exposing weaknesses such as nepotism, corruption, lack of transparency, and weak governance. The crisis forced system changes across the region, although not to the extent foreseen by many Western observers.

The crisis also had a number of consequences for the U.S. perception of Asia, among them a misplaced vindication of the American business model, which was benefiting at the time from a prospering economy and a rising technology boom at home. This is one reason why the advancement of China was not being noticed at the time. China on its part interpreted its ability to withstand the crisis as a reminder that too high a dependence on the global economy was risky and that growth in global markets had to go hand in hand with continuous development in its domestic market. At the same time, it became apparent that Chinese firms, like their Asian counterparts, needed to continue to develop the skills that would make them competitive in a global economy.

China and India: A Tale of Two Nations

Decades ago, India was mentioned together with China as two giants whose rise would shake the global economy. The forecast has been only half true so far. India stumbled time and time again, just when it seemed that it was finally getting serious about reform and about retreating from stifling government regulation and protectionism. More recently, India has been in the news again, this time with tales of economic restructuring, rapid growth, foreign outsourcing, and renewed interest on the part of foreign investors. India's successes, especially in software, have gained visibility, even a prediction that India will catch up with or overtake China.[2]

There are quite a few similarities between India and China. The two nations have enormous populations (roughly 1.3 billion in China and 1 billion in India) and a history as old and proud civilizations that have fallen on hard times and stagnation brought about by a centrally planned autarkic economy with correlates like rampant corruption. Both countries have a multi-million people strong Diaspora with the potential to assist in the country's development, the Chinese Diaspora with capital and business know-how, and the Indian with education, business experience, and advanced technological knowledge. Both nations have been working to liberate their economies from the shackles of socialist control, although ironically it is Communist China (which admittedly started earlier in this round) rather than democratic India that is far ahead in freeing its economy from planning rigidities and a regulatory maze. Both managed to attract some of the most lucrative investment of all—technology research and development—bringing about a debate in the U.S. as to whether this jeopardizes or facilitates U.S. technological leadership.

Several advantages of India are often cited. First, it has been a democracy for over 50 years. This is an advantage from a Western perspective that ties economic progress to democratization, although so far, the Chinese experience seems to challenge this belief. Because of its political structure, China is able to move quickly, whereas a democratic India often gets bogged down in political infighting. A second advantage of India cited is English, which is an official language in the country, while many Chinese are still struggling with it (although urban areas are making quick progress). Japan's example suggests, however, that command of English is helpful but not a prerequisite for entering global markets. So far, English has helped India in areas where the benefit of language ability is obvious, such as in call centers, as well as in software, where it's combined with strong engineering capability. A third advantage of India is a more sophisticated and relatively independent legal and financial system as well as greater transparency in governance. At least in the eyes of a foreign investor, transparency and separation of powers are admittedly a plus, although rampant corruption in both nations lowers the actual benefit accrued from it. In any event, this advantage has proven insufficient so far to redirect the flow of the investment dollars. Finally, India developed a middle class earlier than China, which is a benefit in terms of market potential and professional skills, but China is now catching up fast.

The case for India catching up, or even overtaking China, is made in a recent *Foreign Policy* article.[3] In addition to citing India's legal, political, and governance advantages, the authors make two related overarching arguments: The first, that China's reliance on foreign investment is both proof of and reason for its underlying weaknesses, and second, that China, unlike India, has not developed world-class enterprises and lacks in entrepreneurial skills. Both arguments are misplaced. Foreign investment in China is a reflection of the country's attractiveness as a market and as an export platform. While foreign-invested enterprises are responsible for as much as half of China's exports, they also play a crucial role in upgrading the country's infrastructure and knowledge base, from which local players also benefit as joint venture partners, or via upgraded human resources and the emergence of supporting industries. Many of these local competitors are now giving the multinationals a run for their money in the Chinese market. The second argument about China lacking entrepreneurial skills is also entirely unfounded. A glimpse into Thailand, Malaysia, the Philippines, and other Asian countries reveals that the Chinese make up much of the entrepreneurial class there. Their involvement in the mainland together with that of entrepreneurs from Taiwan and Hong Kong serve as a model for the many indigenous mainland entrepreneurs we see today. Finally, the authors make the case that while India has world-class companies, such as Infosys and Wipro, China has none. Wrong again. Lenovo (formerly Legend) a home-grown manufacturer, has more than a quarter of the Chinese personal computer market, which is about four times Dell's market share. Haier, a leading appliance manufacturer, sells into international markets and now manufactures in the United States. In telecommunications, Huawei Technologies and UTStarcom, among others, are already forces to be reckoned with in developing markets and are beginning to be a factor in developed markets as well. This is without mentioning successful Greater China conglomerates such as Taiwan's Acer or Hong Kong's Hutchison Whampoa, which is one of the largest diversified conglomerates in the world.

Up to now, China's growth rate has been much higher than India's even over the last decade, when India has been reforming. China's growth pace is still higher today, although the gap has been narrowing. Foreign investment in India remains a fraction (less than 10 percent) of the Chinese figure, although it is likely to grow if investors, who have burned their fingers repeatedly in that market, are convinced that the changes this time are for real and that anti-foreign sentiments will not flare up again. While China has many weaknesses, it has made great strides in building its infrastructure and streamlining its regulations. In democratic India, the government continues to play an often-stifling role. Finally, China is globally competitive in a variety of industries, from textiles to appliances, while India is gaining in a narrow range—in particular software, back-office operations, and call centers. This makes India's presence felt in the outsourcing market but does not necessarily translate into a country-wide impact, which is a critical issue in a poverty-stricken nation.

All this is not to say that India will not eventually become a major global player or that it will not compete with China in global markets. To do so, India will have to overcome a number of hurdles. These include geo-politics—in particular its conflict with Pakistan over Kashmir (China has a problem with Taiwan, but it is largely of China's own making, which means that it can easily contain it), a history of broken promises that makes foreign investors nervous, and an underlying resentment of foreign investment, which China has already put behind it. (In addition to physical attacks against a Coca Cola bottling point, India has seen violent attacks and a smear campaign against U.S. fast food chains.) India will also have to liberalize its economy and fix its infrastructure, areas in which China has already made substantial progress. Finally, while India has a thriving overseas community, its Diaspora lacks capital and the will to massively invest in the country. Most importantly, India does not have a Taiwan and a Hong Kong to serve not only as models but also as economic launching points for reform. (For instance, the first economic zones opened for investment in China were in proximity to Hong Kong or Taiwan.)

For these reasons, India is unlikely to catch up with China any time soon, although it will affect certain knowledge-intensive sectors of the global economy—notably software—more than China. More importantly perhaps, India has strengths that are complementary to China, as the booming trade between the two countries suggests. India already provides competitively priced inputs (such as steel) to the fast growing Chinese economy, bolstering its capacity and cost structure. Down the road, India may also begin to absorb investment and growth from a more expensive China; however, the Chinese hinterland has such vast reservoirs of human capital that it can absorb rising costs in its eastern seaboard by way of employee migration, subcontracting, and the like before it would have to ship production to India, Vietnam, or other cheaper competitors. If and where this were to happen, it would hardly provide relief to those sectors who will bear the brunt of the Chinese impact in developed markets and in the other developing markets that are losing ground to China.

4

From Socks to Aircraft

The young consumer often thinks of China as a toy dreamland. He may also have noted the Made in China label on his parents' shoes, clothing, and luggage. China is a world leader in those labor-intensive products but is also the leading global maker of cell phones and a major producer of computer chips, telecommunications, and one day, cars and commercial airplanes. It manufactures military aircraft, has assembled commercial airliners, and is developing regional jets. Chinese firms are determined to ascend the technology ladder, climbing from among the ranks of the imitators, followers, and contractors to become independent developers and pace setters. China's goal, and that of its government, is not merely to catch up with the major industrialized powers but to overpass them. No other developing country has set its sights so high, and none, with the possible exception of Singapore, has laid such a detailed road map designed to take it there. A signal of China's ambitions are its new standards in mobile phones and video compression standards (the Enhanced Versatile Disk, or EVD, that will challenge the DVD), which, while based on licensed foreign technology, are set to enable a technological leapfrogging, and in the meantime, cap technology payments to the foreign firms who still account for the bulk of innovation. Newly proposed wireless security standards for electronic chips are intended to do even more, essentially forcing foreign makers to disclose (and unwittingly transfer) proprietary technological information.

China's attitude toward technology is rooted in a long and complex history; a carefully scrutinized record of emerging economies that have managed rapid technological absorption, in particular Japan and the tigers; and a nascent understanding of the role technology plays in today's increasingly knowledge-intensive economy, including the challenge of applying it in "the real world." To climb the technology ladder, China needs to overcome the absence of a science tradition, improve the transparency that is vital for knowledge dissemination and cross-fertilization, and develop financial and venture capital systems to foster innovation. China's successive regimes were obsessed with stability and order rather than with innovation and progress, and the central planning system left a legacy of excessive compartmentalization across scientific areas and between them and the enterprise. The country's plentiful and low-paid human resources are a competitive edge, but they can also be viewed as a disincentive for the productivity improvements that often drive innovation. At the same time, China is seriously short of people who can do basic research on the one hand and science application on the other.

To overcome these hurdles and achieve its lofty ambitions, China is leveraging a huge wave of foreign investment, learning from the global technology leaders while making sure their advanced knowledge is shared with indigenous companies, and often turning a blind eye when the technology is simply "borrowed." It is introducing fundamental changes to its education and research infrastructure and is enticing its students abroad to come back. China is also utilizing its built-in advantage of not having sunk investment in second-generation technologies to try to leapfrog industrialized nations, and it is investing heavily in cutting-edge areas such as biotechnology and nanotechnology. It is also working hard to coordinate the disjointed efforts across technology producers and users.

As the world's leading developer and exporter of technology, the United States has more at stake in the technology game than most industrialized nations. According to OECD and World Bank figures, in

2000 the U.S. received more than $36 billion in technology receipts (payments made for technology purchase and usage rights, such as licensing) versus payments of roughly $16 billion, for a net surplus of more than $20 billion. By comparison, technological powerhouse Germany's technology balance shows a deficit of almost $5 billion, while Japan's surplus is roughly $5 billion. The U.S., therefore, has the most to lose from uncompensated use of technology through mandatory transfer, counterfeiting, and piracy. Its leadership position also means that leakage of technology and know-how to China or other foreign competitors represents a greater risk to the competitive advantage of the United States than to other nations.

The Technology Legacy

China's technological ambitions are rooted in a long and contradictory record: a thousand-year tradition of technological invention that saw no continuity; military defeat and humiliation that exposed the country's technological lag in the nineteenth and twentieth centuries and haunted the national psyche; and failing attempts to innovate by decree fashioned after the Soviet Union model in the second part of the twentieth century. These experiences—both achievements and failures—still shape China's aspirations and fears concerning technological development, its vision of science, its enterprise role, the obstacles it faces, and its strategy for moving forward.

Inventions But No Science

China's roster of technological achievements before and during the Imperial rule is among the most impressive in ancient times. It includes inventions that have literally changed the world, among them paper, gunpowder, the compass, and the abacus. The Chinese were the first to develop printing and iron casting, the first to use paper money, and the first to launch fireworks and fly kites. They also made major advancements in math and astronomy. Through long stretches of history, China was the most technologically advanced nation in the world.

Despite its impressive invention record, Imperial China failed to develop formal science, which prevented continuous technological development and undermined a diffusion of its inventions into broader spheres of life—particularly its economy. Technological skills were repeatedly downplayed, and, with minor exceptions especially during the Song dynasty, were not fully incorporated into the examination system that screened candidates for future bureaucratic positions. Technical experts, even in such crucial realms as control of water resources, were employed at the prerogative of Imperial officials with generalist training and never gained the prestige and power of officialdom. China had no ideological, administrative, or economic infrastructure to support technological innovation or to disseminate the new knowledge to economic or military activities. This legacy would come to haunt China when it collided with the technologically superior West.

The Price of Falling Behind

China's military defeats in the nineteenth and twentieth centuries exposed the country's technological weaknesses and revealed that the price to be paid for falling behind technologically in the new global era was enormous. The humiliating defeat in the opium war made it clear that the technology slip translated into an inability to develop and produce the modern weapons that have turned out to be essential to becoming an effective combatant. China could no longer rely on sheer numbers of conscripts or creative generals to defend against the enemy; and could no longer assume that prevailing foreign powers would simply be absorbed and assimilated into its cultural milieu. To catch up, China had to set aside its feeling of superiority and start learning from the foreigners who had successfully put China's own inventions—gunpowder and the compass—to use in gunboat diplomacy and international commerce. Japan's success in importing modern technology and putting it to effective use in the Russo-Japanese war demonstrated that it was possible to absorb Western technologies without losing one's national character. The failure of Nationalist China to halt the Japanese onslaught in the 1930s proved, however, that absorbing technology was not a simple task and that Western style governance, in and of itself, was not a guarantee, and perhaps even a hindrance, to the achievement of technological and military parity. If China were to become strong again, it needed not only to aggressively court modern technologies, but also to learn how to develop its own and how to apply them in the real world.

Technology by Decree: The Central Planning Legacy

Following the establishment of the People's Republic of China (PRC) in 1949, China embarked on a massive technology transfer from the Soviet Union. Although a technology borrower from the West and the defunct Third Reich, the Soviet Union had nevertheless displayed an ability to put the technology to use as well as engage in independent technological development in priority areas (mostly national security related), which were injected with massive amounts of capital and priority allocation of human and other resources. Innovation, to the extent that it happened, was dictated from above, with specialized research institutions put to work on projects assigned priority by the upper bureaucracy, a model that Chinese, with their Imperial legacy, were quite comfortable with.

Technology transfer from the Soviet Union was interrupted by Chairman Mao when he feuded with his former comrades and embarked on the disastrous Great Leap Forward. Launched in 1958, the campaign pushed technology away from large-scale enterprises toward amateurish operations in the countryside, resulting in economic chaos and massive starvation. China then retreated to its previous technological order, but marks remained: Technological institutes, like all major enterprises, were duplicated in multiple provinces so they could survive a foreign attack. A few years later, Mao embarked on a second campaign, the Cultural Revolution, which, among other things, targeted the "technocrats" and "elitists" who were holding China's technological infrastructure together. While espousing a "Red and Expert" ideal, Mao saw little value in technical expertise and was convinced that mass power would conquer any knowledge deficiency. China's military successes during the Korean War, although achieved at tremendous human cost, convinced Mao that his approach would lead China to economic, as well as military, successes; however, others in the Chinese leadership managed to insulate the military from the worst of the ideological onslaught. The military establishment continued to do the bulk of the country's research work, concentrating on showcase projects devoid of any economic or commercial considerations. By the 1980s, China, largely an agricultural economy and with an industry reliant on 1950s technology, was a member of the exclusive club of satellite-launching nations.

China of the mid 1970s had the contours of a technological infrastructure, albeit limited and fragmented. While lagging by decades behind the West as well as the Soviet Union, the country had basic technological capabilities and the ability to do industrial applications. This was especially true in heavy industry, where China developed considerable skills in utilizing, servicing, and adapting older technologies and in selected regions—in particular Shanghai—which would later become a driver in the nation's modernization. Technical expertise survived, but in an extremely narrow form and without the ability to connect across different specializations, let alone place them in the context of industrial application. Innovation was still supposed to happen by decree, in areas the government designated as a priority, through a vast network of research institutes, each with a narrowly defined mission and little if any contact with each other, with working enterprises, and with the outside world. The time range of science and technology plans (typically 10–12 years, double the 5-year-long economic plans) reflected not only the Communist penchant for long-term planning, but also little understanding of the fast pace of modern science and the rapid adjustments it necessitated.

Climbing the Technology Ladder

The start of reform in 1979 was accompanied by a slow and incremental rise in openness and transparency. The opening brought home the reality that following decades of Communist rule and the "lost decade" of the Cultural Revolution, China was now further behind the developed world as well as the four Asian tigers than at almost any time since the fall of the Empire. If the Korean War seemed to suggest that throwing in massive numbers of troops could match a rival's advanced technology, new skirmishes with Vietnam exposed military weaknesses, this time against a smaller Asian nation but one with an arsenal of more modern Soviet weapons. Deng Xiaoping and his allies identified technological progress as key to modernization, a ticket to military power and to economic growth and prosperity, without which the then fragile reform effort would have stumbled. It was also evident that the reformers would have to tread carefully in introducing, and especially in utilizing, technology for both ideological and practical reasons. For instance, it made little sense to rush automation and other productivity enhancements into the overstaffed state-owned enterprises, since this would, at least in the short run, increase an already considerable national underemployment and trigger unrest.

The Chinese leadership began its technology upgrade by allocating then precious foreign currency to the wholesale importation of manufacturing lines that were shipped stock and barrel from the West. Most of the imported lines were based on old-line technologies, which Western manufacturers were happy to part with. The relative backwardness of the imported lines was not a problem; after all, they were advanced compared to the Chinese standards of the time, easier to master by local engineers and technicians, and could be more easily serviced using existing skill sets and the available blueprints. The problem was rather, as the Chinese soon discovered, that it was insufficient to import a production line without making fundamental changes to the way the technology was utilized—in particular, the manner in which enterprises were to absorb, manage, and apply it.

The experience in importing complete systems provided an important lesson that would not be soon forgotten. China realized that if it wanted to advance, it needed to shift toward the importation of core equipment as part of a broader transformation from a perception of the enterprise as a collection of narrow technical skills to one that emphasized integrative and synergistic capabilities. Exhibit 4-1 shows China's gradual retreat from the importation of complete production lines between 1994 and 2002, replacing them with technology licensing and transfer, consultation and service agreements, computer software, joint venture production, and cooperative production.

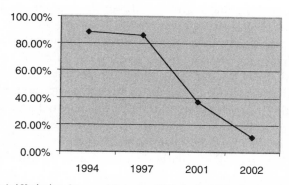

Source: China Statistical Yearbook on Science and Technology 2002; data for 1994 and 1997 are from the Chinese Ministry of Science and Technology, 1999.

Exhibit 4-1   China's Imports of Complete Equipment and Key Equipment Sets (% of All Technology Imports).

Leveraging Foreign Investment

Since foreigners had been shown to have the superior knowledge and hence the military and economic upper hand, it was necessary to learn from them, but it was vital that learning did not "contaminate" China's culture and society in the process. China continued to look for ways to adopt "foreign technologies without foreign values" until the modern-day reform period. It was then that the leadership resolved to suspend its resentment of things foreign, as long as those proved useful; in Deng Xiaoping's words, the color of the cat did not matter as long as it could catch mice. Foreign investment was accorded a key role in technology transfer, and one of the first things that the reformist leadership did was enact a joint venture law that gave priority to technology-intensive investment and required the taking of a Chinese partner. The idea was simple yet globally proven: Joint ventures are an effective means for transferring knowledge comprehensively (to be distinguished from the narrow transfer of production lines, technology purchasing, or licensing) and are less sensitive to nationalist sentiments than operations fully owned by a foreign entity. The reliance on cooperative ventures as a technology transfer vehicle followed the experience of Japan, which insisted on local partner participation in most foreign investment projects during a critical period in its development (1962–1974), relaxing the requirement only when a foreign partner had an especially attractive technology and a strong bargaining position, as was the case with IBM and Texas Instruments.

Parallels notwithstanding, China differed from other technology-hungry recipients of foreign investment in a number of ways, some of which related to the timing of its ascent, others not. First, thanks to the increased attractiveness of its domestic market going forward, China was able to obtain technology on a scale unprecedented for a developing nation, culminating in the establishment of research and development (R&D) centers, the epitome of technology transfer. Second, China was able to leverage its "seller's market" environment to pitch one investor against another and even agree to multiparty technology exchanges. For instance, Chinese automotive companies are in the enviable position of having simultaneous joint venture agreements with rival foreign competitors, (such as Guangzhou Automotive with Honda and Toyota), something the latter have never agreed to do anywhere else. This arrangement enables the Chinese partner to learn "best practices" from both competitors and be the only one in the three-player network to have access to all others. Also, unlike other developing country firms at this stage of development, Chinese firms have started taking an equity position in overseas investment of advanced technology players (such as SAIC in Korean-based venture GM-Daewoo), opening yet another channel for technology access.

Technology Transfer Incentives

To bolster the transfer of technology via foreign investment, special preferences and incentives were provided to technology-intensive ventures. Those who were ready to transfer more cutting-edge technologies and to hand in the underlying capabilities were amply rewarded: They were granted permission to locate in the most desirable areas; given preferential governance and equity terms; provided with prolonged tax holidays and duty exemptions; and, perhaps most importantly, given preferential access or the promise of access to the much-coveted domestic market. These preferences have survived 25 years of reform, multiple rounds of World Trade Organization (WTO) accession negotiations, and occasional pressure by China trade partners.

Today, of the five "encouraged" areas in China's Industrial Guidance on Foreign Direct Investment that receive the highest incentive level, three include the wording "new technology" and the fourth is about meeting the standards of the international marketplace, clearly a technology-driven imperative. (The fifth encourages investment in China's Western regions.) In contrast, projects that involve the mere importation of foreign technology (that is, no "real" technology transfer) are on the "restricted" list.[1] During its WTO membership negotiations, China managed to avoid an explicit commitment to sever the link between foreign investment and technology transfer, although the agreement is supposed to make it more difficult to make the link. A 2003 report on China's WTO compliance notes that "…some of the revised laws and regulations continue to 'encourage' technology transfer, without formally requiring it" and that a new draft policy on the automotive industry sets specific targets for the use of domestic technology. (Despite market liberalization, targets still count, and more so in strategic or "pillar" industries such as automotive, petrochemicals, and machinery.[2])

The incentive to transfer technology is especially salient in high-priority areas such as electronic chips. China, already Intel's biggest customer, wants to reduce its dependence on foreign suppliers for this most technology-intensive part of the product. To do that, it created a rebate system that the United States is now appealing at the WTO: While the value added tax (VAT) levied on imported integrated circuits is 17 percent, a rebate brings it down to 11 percent for locally produced but foreign designed circuits and to 3–6 percent (most often 3) for those designed and produced in China.[3] In a global industry in which labor costs play a relatively minor role, such incentives make a difference and encourage foreign firms to transfer more design to China. In recent years, China has become bolder in its technology transfer demands from foreign investors. A retired executive recently recalled how General Electric conceded key technology to Chinese competitors to win a large turbine bid.[4] While GE managed to retain the most confidential parts of the production process and is adamant that by the time the Chinese are capable of independent production, it will be far ahead with newer technologies, it is clear that at least the second tier of foreign firms is at risk of ceding key capabilities, which will hamper their long-term competitiveness.

In the meantime, the incentives encouraging technology transfer seem to have worked. The share of labor-intensive product lines among Foreign Invested Enterprises (FIEs) declined from 50.42 percent in 1995 to 41.44 percent in 1999. During the same time period, the share of capital-intensive enterprises increased from 22.73 to 25.35 percent, while the share of technology-intensive enterprises rose from 26.86 to 33.21.[5] Today, foreign enterprises account for three quarters of China's sales of technology-related products abroad and, according to some estimates, more than 85 percent of its high-technology exports. As a whole, China is still a fairly minor player in high-tech exports. In 1998 (the most recent figures available), the country exported about $30 billion worth of high-tech goods, versus about $190 billion for the United States, $90 billion for Japan, and $60 billion for the United Kingdom. The Chinese are moving up, however (their high-tech exports were below $5 billion in 1990) and, considering their limited ability to innovate, they must rely on the technology leaders—especially the United States—for knowledge transfer.

Learning from the Barbarians

Technology transfer from foreign investors (or any technology transfer for that matter) depends not only on the willingness of foreigners to transfer but also on the ability of locals to absorb it. It is often argued that China is not ready to absorb advanced technology, but the argument does not rest on solid evidence. A recent study by Peter Buckley and his associates shows that with the exception of investment by overseas Chinese, foreign investment in China generated considerable technology spill-over, which collective firms, although not state-owned enterprises, are able to utilize.[6] If we accept that the share of the state sector in the economy will continue to decline (it now accounts for less than 30 percent of gross domestic product [GDP] versus more than half in 1990), and most indications are that it will, then China will be increasingly able to absorb and apply the technology it receives from foreign multinationals.

Domestic players are now emerging in the most advanced areas. Chinese suppliers, who were not represented at all in the local market for Central Office Switches in 1987, gained a 10 percent market share by 1992 and a 43 percent share by 2000. The rest of the market was held by joint venture companies, while direct imports decreased from 89 percent of the market in 1987 to 54 percent in 1992 and 0 in 2000.[7] In electronic chip fabrication, China is awash with start-ups. Those are often funded and provided expertise by Taiwanese entities but are quickly evolving into full-fledged operations from design to sales.

Indigenous Innovation: Still a Dream

The priority given to technology-intensive foreign investment is also a direct result of China's failure to establish, so far, an effective indigenous network of technological innovation. While the number of patent applications and granted patents in China almost doubled between 1994 and 1999, the share of foreign nationals among them has actually increased to close to 20 percent, a figure higher than in most industrialized countries.[8] Innovation patents were much more likely to be granted to foreigners than to Chinese nationals. The situation does not look much better as far as foreign patent registrations are concerned. According to the OECD figures, Chinese nationals filed merely 200 patent applications in 1995 and 299 in 1997. While these numbers are likely pulled down by funding constraints, they are still extremely small.

This leaves foreign investment and the repatriation of Chinese scientists as major vehicles for technological innovation until China is in a position to build up a domestic innovation network. There are signs that indigenous capabilities are developing; for instance, the new R&D centers established by foreign firms have already generated dozens of patents by Chinese scientists, but China has a long way to go before it becomes an innovation hub. As Exhibit 4-2 shows, only a miniscule percentage of the patents granted to Chinese are for invention, which makes up the bulk of patents granted to foreigners.

Exhibit 4-2   Types of Patents Granted to Foreigners (2001).

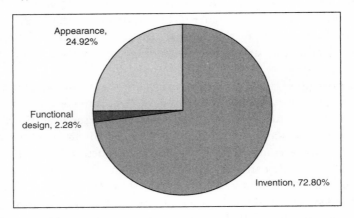

Types of Patents Granted to Chinese (2001).

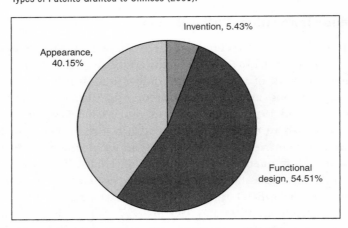

Source: National Bureau of Statistics and Ministry of Science and Technology, 2002-2003.

Developing Research Capabilities

While China's R&D expenditure more than tripled between 1991 and 1999, the growth was largely a function of economic growth. As a percentage of GDP, science and technology (S&T) and R&D expenditure went from 1.8 and 0.7 in 1991 to 1.57 and 0.83, respectively, in 1999. Basic research remained a relative rarity, accounting for a mere 5 percent of R&D expenditure in the 1995–1998 period versus 25 percent for applied research and 70 percent for experimental development.

To ensure that China gains the most important technological capability—the ability to do its own research—establishing R&D centers on Chinese soil has become a major priority for the Chinese authorities. A major factor in General Motors winning over Ford in the hotly contested Shanghai investment was its willingness to establish a large R&D center and transfer up-to-date technology to that center. Today, the list of foreign firms with China-based R&D centers includes the likes of Oracle, Siemens, Lucent, Nokia, Nortel, Agilent, IBM, and Hewlett Packard. All in all, more than two hundred such centers have opened up.

Some Western observers argue that the importance of the centers has been exaggerated, that they are not involved in actual innovation but are limited to implementation and especially product adaptation to local conditions. This may be true for now as Chinese staff still struggle with the idea of basic research on the one hand and enterprise linkages on the other. However, this may not be the case for long. Even adaptation research develops skills that can later be used for "core development" tasks. Besides, multinational enterprises have been consolidating and rationalizing their far-flung R&D centers and increasing their R&D outsourcing, suggesting further growth in scope and depth for the Chinese centers.

Already, U.S. affiliates in China are among the most R&D-intensive overseas affiliates. National Science Foundation (NSF) data show that by 2000, China was the eleventh largest host for overseas R&D expenditure by U.S. firms, up from thirtieth in 1994. A measure of R&D intensity, R&D-to-gross-product ratios among U.S. China-based Foreign Invested Enterprises or FIEs (wholly and majority owned) increased from 1 percent in 1994 to 9.2 percent in 2000. China-based U.S. affiliates invest more in R&D compared to U.S. affiliates in other countries. For the aggregate of all U.S. affiliates abroad, the ratio is a mere 3.3 percent, just over one-third the figure for China. At over 2 percent, the average published by the Organization for Economic Cooperation and Development (OECD) is even lower. In dollar terms, R&D expenditure by U.S. affiliates in China rose from 7 million in 1994 to over half a billion in 2000.[9]

To ensure that technology is transferred even where foreign manufacturing is absent or not welcome, research partnerships are encouraged. By the end of the century, Chinese firms had established 90 such partnerships, about three times the number for India and more than Taiwan, Hong Kong, and Singapore combined. Among the leaders in establishing such partnerships were Sinopec, with seven; CATIC (China Aerotech), with four; and China Aerospace, with three international partnerships.[10] In addition, many business alliances had a significant R&D component. Based on Thomson Financial data, the NSF identified 105 such partnerships between U.S. and Chinese firms in the 1990 to 2001 period.[11] Another, emerging venue for obtaining technology is the procurement of R&D abroad either directly or by the overseas subsidiaries of Chinese firms. There is some evidence that this is occurring, although for now it's on a small scale.

Upgrading China's "Humanware"

A few years into the reform effort, a Chinese official told me that the problem in China was not hardware or software but "humanware." What he meant was that without upgrading the human resource base, it was futile—or at least of limited value—to invest in new equipment or modernize processes and routines. The country clearly had a long way to go. In 2000, China had 459 scientists and engineers doing R&D work for every million people, equivalent to about 10 percent the U.S. ratio. Chinese scientists published about 9,000 science and technology journal articles that year, compared to 166,000 by U.S. scholars. Clearly, this was not for lack of attention or interest: Chinese science and engineering students represented 43 percent of those in tertiary education versus 19 percent in the U.S.[12] The problem was less in the numbers and more in the content and level of what they have learned as well as in their ability to apply that knowledge within an enterprise context.

To improve its "humanware," China employs two strategies. The first strategy is undertaking a fundamental reform of the educational system. The second strategy involves a major effort to bring home the many scientists and engineers who have left the country to pursue educational opportunities in industrialized nations. This repatriation is seen as a way to bring cutting-edge capabilities while changing the organizational culture within Chinese research organizations and enterprises, providing a potentially potent combination of exogenous and endogenous knowledge.

Transforming the Educational System

The Chinese leadership started from a dismal point, where an educational system that left a lot to be desired during the best of times was literally torn apart during the Cultural Revolution. With some of China's brightest scientists and professors working the fields in the countryside, the technological community was cast away from the outside world and missed on the technological advances of the time. It also lost its facilities, equipment, and motivation to conduct scientific work. The reforms have gradually restored the educational infrastructure, its importance cemented (as is often the case in China) with the establishment of a high-level committee: a working group on science and education, chaired by the Chinese premier.

Traditionally, education in China has been the reserve of the select few. The Imperial examination system screened a relatively small number of candidates, and few of those passed and became eligible for bureaucratic appointment. The Communist system, while professing to equalize education, permitted only a small fraction of the brightest and well connected to attend institutes of higher education. It was relatively late into the reform effort that authorities came to realize that sustainable technological progress required broadening the higher education base. By 2000, gross enrollment in "tertiary education" stood at 11 percent—twice as many as in 1990. Still, this represented a mere 2.4 percent of total enrolment in education. In comparison, the average enrollment in tertiary education in the OECD countries is 14 percent, despite the fact that those nations allocate a similar portion (22 percent) of their overall educational expense to higher education.[13]

What has not changed in China over the years is the high regard accorded to education and the readiness of families to invest enormous resources to promote the educational success of their offspring. In Imperial times, a series of arrangements (such as the collectively toiled "book lamp fields") funneled resources to support the studies of the most promising clan members. Now, it was the turn of families to support their "little emperors" (the term used in China to denote the pampered children born under the one-child policy). This explains why despite a relatively modest national expenditure on education (less than 3 percent of GDP, which is lower than that of several developing countries), there has been an impressive expansion of educational activities, many of which are paid in part or in full by the parents.

Another important reform concerned curriculum content and pedagogy. Ironically, while both Confucius and Mao advocated the use of generalists, a central planning system and lack of transparency (virtually anything the government did was classified at some level) created narrow specialists with little understanding of how their jobs were nested in broader systems and processes. One of China's main problems during the early reform years was unawareness of the need for integration across functions and departments; therefore, a key education initiative has been to cluster fields of study around an industry, especially if it is considered advanced, such as telecommunications.

Still another change in the educational system was increased internationalization. This involved importation of content (such as translation of foreign textbooks)—mostly in science, technology, law, and management—and the establishment of exchange programs for students and faculty. (China had almost 45,000 foreign students from 164 countries in 2000.) A key element in the internationalization effort, devised to prepare Chinese students for the global economy, was the encouragement of study abroad, especially in science and engineering. By 2000, Chinese students were attending universities in more than 100 countries across the globe.[14] In the United States, Chinese students became the largest group.

Finally, China's top universities and research institutions (the government designated a "top 100" group, eligible for special funding and research initiatives) benefited from the help of many multinationals, which wanted to show good will while preparing a cadre of skilled graduates they could use. The importance of this cooperation for a country that started its university reform the same way it started its manufacturing revival—by wholesale importation of the textbooks used in America's premier institutions—cannot be overestimated. The multinationals not only help in providing up-to-date curriculums and funding new equipment, but crucially in providing a linkage between research and application—a key weakness of the Chinese system and one that is even pinpointed to be in need of improvement in the United States.

The Return of the "Turtles"

The strategy of sending students abroad was initially suspected by the more conservative elements in the Chinese leadership. No one could guarantee the students would return (indeed, most did not), and those who did were suspected of importing undesirable ideas, such as democracy. Eventually, however, a lower level of paranoia combined with a realization of how difficult it was to launch innovation from within convinced the leadership that here was an opportunity they could not miss: The "turtles" (as they are called in China to denote the tendency of the species to return to its birthplace) could play a key role in China's technological transformation. A recent reception for returning students by the Chinese president at Beijing Great Hall of the People shows how much the attitude has changed.

The stakes are huge. The United States alone counted almost 65,000 Chinese students in the 2002–2003 academic year, with 36,000 more from Taiwan and Hong Kong. In total, according to a Singapore-based scholar, Cong Cao, 160,000 PRC students went abroad in 2002.[15] Many of those students are specializing in technology-related areas. According to the National Science Foundation, more than 21,000 Chinese students have earned science and engineering doctorates in the United States in the period from 1986 to 1998, accounting for 7.5 percent of all science and engineering doctorates awarded during that period.[16] The China contingent is especially visible at the doctoral level, which encompasses skills critical in research and development. In 2002, according to the NSF, 2,395 students from China were awarded science and engineering doctorates. In addition, 469 and 42 students from Taiwan and Hong Kong, respectively, also received such degrees. By comparison, India had 678 graduates, about a quarter the Greater China number.[17]

True, 85 percent of the 1986 to 1998 students planned to stay in the U.S., and 48 percent of 1998 graduates accepted offers from U.S. employers by graduation time; however, this is down from the 88 percent figure reported in 1995. According to Cong Cao, Chinese estimates for actual return rates were considerably higher, ranging from 25 to 30 percent. It is reasonable to assume that as China continues to modernize, many graduates will be enticed back home. This has happened before in South Korea, where only 11 percent of science and technology PhDs were working in America in 1995.[18] Given the large number of Chinese graduates, even a modest increase in the repatriation rate will bring home hundreds of doctoral-level Chinese scientists and engineers who could disseminate their expertise to others. Such an increase is not unreasonable to expect given the perception of increased opportunities back home and the array of government-sponsored programs to entice them, including, for instance, the National Science Fund for Distinguished Young Scholars, the One Hundred Talent Program, and the Cheung Kong Scholar Program.[19] Many of the programs target not only new graduates, but also senior scientists. (The Cheung Kong program is partially modeled after Singapore, which allows researchers joint appointments in foreign and domestic institutions.) There is also evidence that more experienced Chinese scientists and engineers are returning, bringing with them not only technological know-how, but also the executive and international savvy that are essential in the global marketplace. Even those who stay can make a contribution to the motherland. In a study cited by the National Science Foundation, H. Choi notes that Asian-born faculty and researchers in the United States—particularly in science and engineering—tend to advise and disseminate information to their home countries.[20]

The results of China's effort to upgrade its educational system while enticing home the best and the brightest are already visible. Data compiled by Jon Sigurdson and Olle Persson show that China's global share of scientific articles rose from 0.63 percent in 1986 to 1.83 in 1997 and 3.54 in 2001. Articles by China-based scholars in the prestigious *Science and Nature* journals rose from 11 in 1986 to 93 in 2001. In material science, China ranked fourth globally in 2001, with a 1.6 percent citation rate (versus 5.5 for the U.S.); in engineering, China was ninth with a respectable 1.5 percent citation rate (versus 3.6 for the U.S.). Progress has been especially impressive in cutting-edge areas such as nanoscience, where China's share rose from 5.5 percent in 1995 to 11.2 percent in 2001, placing it seventh in the world; still, its citation rate was low.[21]

Bringing Technology to the Enterprise

A fundamental problem in China's R&D legacy has been the lack of an infrastructure for diffusing technology, whether acquired or indigenously developed, to where it was needed—namely the enterprise. Having learned the importance of such dissemination, the government established "high-technology zones" in the late 1980s and devised schemes such as the "Torch Plan," targeted at getting technology research into the production environment.[22] While the plans have managed a measurable level of success, they have not changed the underlying problems. Enterprises have started taking on more R&D work, but they have been inefficient in that task. While generating 54 percent of the applications for domestic invention patents in the 1996–1999 period (increasingly generated with its own funds), the enterprise sector accounts for merely 23 percent of the domestic invention patents granted during the same period. The gap suggests that Chinese firms are far from mastering the innovation process and will continue to be reliant on the continuing flow of technology from both foreign and indigenous sources for the foreseeable future.

That said, Chinese firms are busy upgrading their R&D capabilities. In large and medium-size enterprises, the proportion of R&D personnel to total employees has grown from 2.6 percent in 1987 to 3.9 percent in 1998, and the share of scientists and engineers among R&D personnel grew from 28.2 percent in 1987 to 54.4 percent in 1998.[23] "Science and Technology enterprises," typically spin-offs or affiliates of research institutions and institutes of higher education, are leading the way. These enterprises, which numbered 70,000 in 1999,[24] are joined by a new breed of university spin-offs that benefit from China's chaotic governance (universities often establish enterprises that have little to do with their core mission) as well as by other start-ups. Rural enterprises are also hoping not to fall behind. In a study of rural enterprises in Jiangsu province, Sun and Wang found that on average, about three quarters of product innovations were internally generated, although often by staff trained in national universities. These enterprises benefited from the phase-out of the government placement system, which assigned college graduates to major enterprises.[25] Nascent technology clusters have also enabled China to obtain some of the agglomeration benefits that have eluded it in the past.

OEM, ODM, OBM

The growth in the R&D and S&T capabilities of Chinese enterprises is intricately related to their attempt to transcend their traditional roles as "factories to the world" and become well-rounded firms able to develop a product and eventually sell it under their own name. Chinese manufacturers typically start as component suppliers to foreign buyers and as Original Equipment Manufacturers (OEMs), like the group of manufacturers who recently agreed to make flat screen television sets for Motorola. Such firms produce to the specifications of foreign firms who distribute and sell the product in their home or other foreign markets or embed it in one of their end products. The arrangement provides Chinese firms with substantial growth opportunities despite limited technological capabilities; no less importantly, it allows them to incrementally upgrade their skills by studying customer requirements and by receiving direct technological support from the buyer in terms of machinery, technical assistance, and the like. A Chinese (or a joint venture) company that supplies components to a U.S. car maker (as is increasingly the case) receives detailed specifications necessary for the production of the components that also tell something about the new product development plans and standards of the buyer. Often, the relationship grows and develops, as in the case of France's Thomson merging its television business with that of China-based TCL, a deal that will inevitably trigger significant technology transfer.

As they gain knowledge and experience, Chinese firms are developing the design capabilities to turn them into Original Design Manufacturers (ODMs)). They can receive a rough sketch of a product and perform the design work in house or in nearby Hong Kong or Taiwan. This was initially true for simple products such as plastic toys but is now expanding to more technology-intensive products with the help of the foreign buyers who find the Chinese designs cheap and of good quality. Chinese firms often say that they are forced to develop design capabilities by the relentless pricing pressure exerted by foreign buyers as well as by domestic competitors, as this enables them to capture some of the higher margins available in design and development. Once the OEMs have developed design capabilities, they are in a position to bypass the middleman and go directly to the end buyer. The shift from an OEM to an ODM requires significant technological upgrading: more and higher-level engineers, mastery of the latest technologies, creative thinking and problem-solving abilities, and an understanding of how the various functions of management relate to each other and to the outside world. These qualities are not found in abundance in China now. That is where educational reform, foreign education, and the transfer of skills from foreign firms to domestic players come in. This explains why those areas are accorded high priority by the Chinese leadership.

Successful Chinese ODMs seek to move up further and become OBMs (Original Branded Manufacturers), although few establish themselves as such from the start. OBMs not only design and manufacture but also sell their products under their own name. (Some, in fact, farm out the manufacturing to other Chinese firms.) So far, a number of Chinese firms (such as Haier and Huawei Technologies) have established recognized brand names abroad. These firms face not only marketing challenges but also the need to develop independent research capabilities by which to differentiate their products. Such firms make a major effort to recruit promising graduates and returnees as well as experienced expatriates, usually on short-term assignments.

Technology as a Freebie

As China remains dependent on foreign technologies, the way in which it procures and pays for new technology is of increasing importance to its future competitiveness, as well as to technology leaders and owners, such as the United States. As long as China's bargaining power remains strong, it is likely to continue to find ways to condition foreign investment on the transfer of technology. The country will also continue to tolerate expropriation of technology and other property rights by way of piracy, counterfeiting, and other violations. This expropriation has been a critical element in keeping development costs down and is one explanation why Chinese manufacturers are able to sell at a cost that seems absurd even when one factors in cheap labor and various rebates and subsidies. Chapter 5, "The Two-Dollar Rolex," discusses the issue of piracy and counterfeiting in greater detail.

5

The Two-Dollar Rolex

O utside China's major hotels, tourists are amused by the sight of Rolex watches being peddled for a few dollars. There is nothing funny, though, about the scale and scope of China's fake products industry or about the ramifications for the manufacturers of the genuine articles, mostly foreign multinationals. In 1998, China's Development and Research Center estimated the sales of pirated and counterfeit products at $16 billion annually; later reports raised the count to between $19 and $24 billion.[1] The real numbers, to the extent that they can be measured accurately, are probably higher: The Chinese government wants to show that the problem is under control, and legitimate firms fear that high counts would lead customers to pass up on the genuine good for fear it is a fake.

Yankee Footprints

China is not the first nation to openly violate intellectual property rights (IPR). It may come as a surprise to many Americans, but the United States, who today leads a global effort to curb IPR violations, was itself a major violator during the nineteenth century. J.K. Rowling, whose last three *Harry Potter* books are bootlegged in China, even though the author is not finished writing them, can take solace in recalling the frustration of Charles Dickens, whose royalty demands were rebuffed by U.S. publishers of the time. When American publishers infringed on the rights of British authors, however, there was not much else that could be copyrighted. The situation today is vastly different. According to the International Intellectual Property Alliance (IIPA), the core U.S. copyright industries accounted for 5.24 percent of U.S. GDP in 2001, or $535.1 billion. From 1977 to 2001, these industries grew at a rate of seven percent annually, more than twice that of the economy as a whole. Employment in this segment grew nearly three times faster than in the national economy and now accounts for 4.7 million U.S. jobs. Exports reached $88.97 billion, more than for the aircraft or automotive sector.[2] Other industries, from pharmaceuticals to electronics, are heavily reliant on property rights to protect huge development costs and brand-building expenditure, as are service providers. IPR underlie the lead of the United States, and to a lesser extent Japan, the European Union (EU), and other developed economies, in technology-intensive sectors and in the knowledge industries of the future. IPR protection is a key element in all free market economies, underpinning the incentive to innovate, develop, invest, and produce. Violations are easier to commit, however: "Digitized" products can be downloaded off the Internet, and disc production machines can be had for a fraction of their price a decade ago. In today's global environment, IPR infringements show up not only as local market losses but also as worldwide forfeiture of revenue and reputation.

The American precedent may yet be followed by China. Compliance and eventual championship of IPR by the United States came after its legal system had matured and its laws became enforceable; however, compliance and vigorous defense did not come about until America emerged as a major producer of copyrighted knowledge, with more to lose from IPR infringement than to gain from evading those rights.

China, too, may become a defender of IPR in due course, but this will not occur until its firms have become technology leaders. This, as the previous chapter illustrates, will not happen any time soon. In the meantime, China continues to get a free ride on the technology and reputation of legitimate, mostly foreign manufacturers, which is tolerated, often supported, and at times, even orchestrated by Chinese authorities, especially at the local level.[3]

Piracy, Counterfeiting, and the Like

Some vocabulary: *Piracy,* or *bootlegging,* refers to the unauthorized production, distribution, or use of a good, design, or technology via unauthorized means, such as copying software, imitating a patented industrial process, or selling a motorcycle based on somebody else's design without permission and compensation. *Counterfeiting,* or the selling of *fake* or *bogus* merchandise, goes a step further by trying to pass the product for an original, as in the sale of an imitation Gucci bag. Some products are amenable to one violation but not another. For instance, it is not feasible to sell a counterfeit Ford Focus, but it is possible to copy its design and to sell component parts under its brand name. Elements of piracy and counterfeiting can also be combined. A Chinese motorcycle manufacturer sells a locally made motorcycle based on a Honda design under the trademark "Nihon Honda," which it registered in Japan. A local beverage maker markets mineral water under its own brand name, but the bottle's appearance is a Perrier look-alike. A variety of other practices, such as reverse engineering, are more difficult to detect and are rampant in China as in other countries.

Piracy, counterfeiting, and their various derivatives cause an enormous damage to the IPR owners who have invested in development and marketing only to find that consumers have substituted a cheaper imitation for the real thing. ABC News recently estimated the losses suffered in China by foreign firms at $20 billion annually. Two out of five foreign manufacturers are losing more than 20 percent of their local revenue, which for a company like Procter & Gamble amounts to $150 million a year. In some product categories, fakes have now taken over from the original as market leaders. For instance, more than half of the motorcycles sold in China are knock-offs of Japanese brands such as Honda and Yamaha. The same is true for products ranging from razor blades and cell phones to chewing gum and shampoo, DVDs, and

Windows XP software (street price: $2). Safety-related products, such as automotive parts and pharmaceuticals, are also fair game: Thomas Boam, a former Minister Counselor at the U.S. Embassy in Beijing, estimates that half of the pharmaceuticals sold in China are from a pirated or counterfeit origin. High-technology items, such as electronic chips, are knocked off as well, modified to accommodate pirated inputs (say, a video game), thus creating a value chain based on piracy.[4] Many imitations are of dubious quality, such as the disposable camera I bought for my son in a five star hotel (which did not offer any other brand) whose shots came back blank from the lab. Others are made surprisingly well and have garnered admiration from brand owners, in some cases even prompting joint ventures with the offenders. Millions of Chinese-made fake products find their way every year to overseas markets from Vietnam and Nigeria to the United States and the EU.

In a world where developing a new car routinely exceeds a billion dollars, piracy and counterfeiting remove a steep barrier to new entrants and allow those falling behind to catch up on the cheap. The expropriation of others' investment in developing and perfecting technologies and processes can yield major cost reductions that in certain instances can outweigh the savings emanating from lower wages. The scale, scope, and timing of China's IPR violations pose a substantial risk for foreign firms, especially those whose competitive advantage lies in knowledge and innovation, as well as for their governments who underwrite much of the research and development (R&D) budget. As the number one producer of new technology, the United States is the most vulnerable on that front. Furthermore, the fat margins of pirated and counterfeit production increasingly attract international crime syndicates, and there are preliminary indications that global terror groups have eyed them as a way to fund their operations.

The Costs and Benefits of Knock-Offs

For the firms who own property rights, the cost of the violations is tremendous. First, there is the direct loss of revenues and market share, sometimes to a point where it is no longer profitable to do business in China. The loss is amplified when the pirated and counterfeit goods are exported to overseas markets. In an industry such as motor vehicles, where margins are razor thin, the spread of bogus components is especially damaging, since "aftermarket" sales produce a much higher profit margin that supports mainline manufacturing. Unable to fund development costs from this revenue stream, the legitimate player may lose its long-term competitiveness. Then, there is a potentially severe damage to reputation as unhappy customers purchase a counterfeit they believe to be genuine and blame the legitimate maker for their trouble. Companies whose products have been counterfeited and pirated also face a potential increase in warranty cost as a fake component can result in system failure, such as engine breakdown. Finally, there is the potential liability and litigation cost when a safety-related product such as a break pad fails, and the legitimate manufacturer is implicated.

Given their technological lead, the losers in the piracy and counterfeiting game are by and large the foreign companies owning the technology or trademark. While a firm does not need to be in China to have its product knocked off, physical presence, especially when combined with substantial technology transfer to multiple parties, may facilitate infringement because it provides others with a close-up look at the intricacies of the production process. A case in point is Yamaha, which estimates that five out of six motorcycles sold under its name in China are bogus, not to mention numerous part designs that find their way to local competitors. The company suspects that its Chinese suppliers have sold its technology to local manufacturers, and estimates that no less than 88 of those now copy its scooter.[5] Reuters reported that Nintendo, the video game maker, put its 2002 losses from piracy at about $650 million, the bulk of which have come from China where 300,000 of its games have been seized in just one series of raids in the southern part of the country. As owners are deprived of their rights, their shareholders, employees, and suppliers all share in the loss. And the U.S., the technology leader and the largest "brand equity" owner, is the first in line (but by no means the only one) to bear the brunt. The direct losses of U.S. IPR owners in copyrighted industries (such as movies) alone in China have been estimated at more than $1.8 annually.[6]

The American experience in shifting from a nineteenth century violator to a twentieth century enforcer indicates that China will eventually crack down on piracy and counterfeiting because it will be in its own interest to do so. That's possible, but it's doubtful it will happen any time soon. First, China has already proven to be a special case: For instance, common economic wisdom suggests that corruption is associated with lower levels of foreign investment, but China, despite its corruption record, is now the world's number one investment destination, the attraction of its market and manufacturing environment sufficient to hold off the adverse impact. Second, as long as China remains far behind on technological innovation and brand recognition, it is in the interest of most of its enterprises to piggyback on the technological know-how and reputation of the original manufacturer without paying for the cost incurred in obtaining them. This "borrowing" represents a tremendous advantage, especially in areas that are capital and technology intensive, such as aircraft, or where reputation plays a particularly important role, such a pharmaceuticals. The savings in research, development, engineering, and advertising costs can be passed on to the consumer in the form of a cheaper price or can be used to increase margins, some of which can then be invested in technological upgrading, which will eventually lower the need for imitation.

The lowering of incentives for innovation and development is often mentioned as a potential drawback of piracy and counterfeiting that applies to local players as well. Without IPR protection, goes the argument, prospects for the emergence of an indigenous, technology-intensive industry will remain slim. This is a reasonable argument, but it is based on the experience of other counties rather than on the special circumstances of the Chinese environment, where the judicial, administrative, and legislative branches remain closely intertwined. My own prediction is that at least in the first phase of China's technological progress, indigenous IPR owners will receive the protection and support of the authorities, while foreign holders will continue to struggle.

An Industry in the Making

Chinese firms are not the only ones to engage in anything from the copying of an art design to industrial espionage. It is the scale, the scope, and brazenness that set China apart and create an impact of major proportions. Although overall rankings are unavailable, various indicators point at China as the undisputed leader in the use, manufacturing, distribution, and exportation of pirated and counterfeit products. In a speech to the National Association of Manufacturers, Thomas Boam, the minister counselor, estimated that between 10 and 30 percent of China's GDP comes from piracy and counterfeiting. By some estimates, pirated and counterfeit goods now account for 15 to 20 percent of retail sales nationally, with some local markets approaching 90 percent. In most "digitized" categories, China's violation rates routinely exceed aggregates of 90 percent, ranging from 94 percent for software to 97 percent for video console games. The rate for audiocassettes is 100 percent.[7] U.S.-based toy firms procure most of their products in China, but many have yet to sell a single product there, and not for lack of demand: Fake versions of their products, often produced next door to their own plant, sell briskly.

All this is taking place in broad daylight, with fake goods outlets spreading up in dusty regional towns, as well as in major metropolises where goods are displayed prominently, offered by street vendors and in trendy establishments. Suppliers are both underground operations and "legitimate" factories. Some use the legitimate part of the business as a front for the sale of lookalike products. Others simply make unauthorized production runs; still others incorporate pirated and counterfeit components sometimes unknowingly. The occasional raid by the central authorities fails to make a dent in the widespread and growing phenomenon. In a testimony before the U.S.-China Commission, David Quam, general counsel of the International Anti Counterfeiting Coalition (IACC), gave the example of an illegal automotive factory that has been raided three times in a 2.5-year period but remains in operation with the same staff and machinery. The activity is underpinned by other corrupt practices, such as bribery and smuggling, and supported by powerful local interests and increasingly by international crime syndicates.

Institutional and Legacy Factors

China's bootlegging operations rely not only on the initiative of brazen entrepreneurs, but also on a special combination of circumstances. A legal system lacking in capabilities, independence, and enforcement; lack of open and independent media; immunity of public officials; lack of transparency in government operations; government power; and low official pay have all been associated with corrupt practices the world over. Add to the mix technical capability and production scale and know-how, and you have an unmatched global piracy and counterfeiting haven. Other potential competitors in the counterfeit industry possess some of those ingredients (India, for instance, has endemic official corruption but also independent media and a professional legal system; Vietnam flaunts IPR but has few capabilities and small scale), but only China has them all. It is here where China's unique combination of a non-democracy and a market economy comes into play.

China's penchant for producing fake goods has sometimes been explained by its culture and tradition, such as the positive role Confucianism has for emulation as an effective way to disseminate normative behavior. The argument is not very convincing, since what Confucius had in mind was the modeling of virtuous behavior; however, there are other legacy elements that have made a difference, such as the lack of independence for the judiciary and, in particular, the autonomy of local authorities from the center expressed in the old saying "The sky is high, and the emperor is far away." This tradition continued under Communist rule, which, like its counterpart regimes, had no respect for IPR in any event. Today, local authorities are dependent on revenues from enterprises that use knocked-off designs, such as China's 100 plus car manufacturers, most of which would be out of business if they had to pay for development costs. Some local jurisdictions are dependent on lucrative trade and distribution centers for bogus goods for much of their income and are reluctant to relinquish those benefits, especially when they find a central government willing to look the other way. With unemployment already a serious economic, social, and political threat, the central authorities are reluctant to take action against an industry that employs millions of people; the unrest that might result is the nightmare of a regime billing itself as a guardian of order and stability. Thus, while many developing countries have been cleaning up their act, China is falling further behind, its occasional efforts lagging behind the progress of violators.

Counterfeiting and piracy are also aided by other corrupt practices—in particular bribe paying—which together form an intricate web. Firms that suffer as a result of piracy must often pay, if not outright bribe, the officials who are supposed to monitor the abuse and enforce rulings. Transparency International's Bribe Payers Index (BPI) places China second highest among the 21 nations included in its survey. Taiwan is in third place, and Hong Kong shares sixth and seventh place; none of the three has signed the OECD Convention against bribery. The Foreign Corrupt Practices Act (FCPA) , which criminalizes the payment of bribes to foreign officials for securing a deal, has put the U.S. at a disadvantage vis-à-vis their foreign rivals, some of whom could even write it off as a business expense; this might be one explanation why the U.S. has exported less to China than other countries. The OECD 1999 agreement on Combating Bribery of Foreign Officials in International Business (CBFOIB) has since been ratified by signatory nations, but it remains to be seen whether it will be enforced.

Another corrupt practice that underpins the manufacturing and flow of bogus goods is smuggling. For all the talk about China as a tightly controlled society, Chinese borders are fairly porous, as the one-time preponderance of cars with right-side steering (smuggled from Hong Kong) demonstrates. Smuggling facilitates the inflow of bogus components and other production inputs from other major violators, such as Vietnam and Malaysia. The products make their way into the Chinese mainland directly or via Hong Kong or Macao, the latter having a reputation for ineffectual monitoring of its waters and a proliferation of organized crime. The porous borders also encourage the outflow of bogus goods into neighboring countries and from there to other overseas markets. Other corruption-related problems, such as lack of transparency and broad nepotism, also support piracy and counterfeiting. These practices reduce the effectiveness of monitoring and enforcement, undermine deterrence, and make the job of pirates and counterfeiters easier.

The Organization of Fake Production

The manufacturing and distribution of bogus products is no longer an isolated activity. Although small, entrepreneurial purveyors of fake goods continue to mushroom, production, sales, and distribution are now large scale, well-financed organized activities. Manufactured goods are packaged professionally to the point that some brand owners have had trouble telling the original from the bogus. The packaging not only minimizes the probability of detection by authorities but also gives the buyer the impression that this is a genuine article, or, at least, a quality knockoff that merits a smaller discount from the original. Packaged products are shipped to order or sent to large wholesale centers, such as the infamous Yiwu town, where prospective retail and wholesale buyers flock to check the merchandise, make purchases or place orders, and arrange for delivery. This increasingly sophisticated supply chain is financed with the revenues obtained from a profitable business (profit margins are much fatter for fakes than for legitimate goods), as well as by new players such as Asian organized crime syndicates who utilize capital obtained from gambling, prostitution, drug trafficking, and the like to expand into this lucrative area. These players bring with them capabilities in the realms of transportation and distribution, as well as in deception and cover-up.

Producers in the fake product industry are a diverse bunch, ranging from a large dedicated facility to the individual who concocts an imitation shampoo at home and outsources the packaging and labeling. Large-scale manufacturers can be state-owned firms, township and village enterprises (TVEs), or private, entrepreneurial firms. Among the participants are legitimate enterprises that resort to bogus production because they have fallen on hard times or because they are pressured to become profitable, which is the case for many in the state sector. Such players, often joint venture partners with a foreign firm, will divert some output without the knowledge of the foreign investor or will run another line using the same designs or equipment. Others are "shadow" enterprises, established for the purpose of fake manufacturing. Some of those evolve into quasi-legitimate players, producing a variant of the knocked-off product. All players share a cost advantage based on zero investment in technology and reputation building, low-cost raw materials and components, and labor cost that is usually below that of legitimate firms. With the fake industry gaining in maturity, players are increasingly differentiated by product quality and appearance, with those up the ladder able to command higher prices. Even some foreign-invested enterprises unwittingly take part in the fake trade by using bogus inputs or selling to an illegitimate assembler.

The know-how is routinely knocked off the foreign investors, who are the main agents of technological innovation, by the employees who have previously worked for the foreign enterprise, the suppliers who received its blueprints and specifications, and the officials who reviewed its proposals and monitored its investment and technology transfer. You don't have to be in China for your products to be copied, however: Chinese executives and entrepreneurs roam international shows and exhibits, looking for anything that can be copied profitably. Ongoing technological advances help in lowering the cost structure of imitators and in creating look-alike products that are often hard to tell from the original.

Pirating "Digitized" Products

The increasingly effortless nature of duplicating digitized products makes industries such as software, recording, and motion pictures especially susceptible to uncompensated use; while abuse is relatively common in many countries, it tends to be of a larger scale and often of a more sophisticated level in China. Exhibit 5-1 shows estimated trade losses from IPR infringement of digitized and printable goods. Note that the numbers reflect only domestic (within China) losses (and therefore exclude losses emanating from the exportation of pirated intellectual property to other countries), and that they refer to only a slice of the overall piracy and counterfeiting industry. (For instance, the numbers do not include the losses suffered by foreign automotive makers when their designs are knocked off.) The numbers also do not include rampant violation of consumer software and the like.

PEOPLE'S REPUBLIC OF CHINA
ESTIMATED TRADE LOSSES DUE TO PIRACY
(in millions of U.S. dollars)
and LEVELS OF PIRACY: 1999-2003

INDUSTRY	1999		2000		2001		2002		2003	
	Loss	Level	Loss	Level	Loss	Level	Loss	Level	Loss	Level
Motion Pictures	120	90%	120	90%	160	88%	168	91%	178	95%
Records & Music	70	90%	70	93%	47	90%	48	90%	286	90%
Business Software Applications	437.2	91%	765.1	94%	1140	92%	1637.3	92%	1593.3[1]	93%[1]
Entertainment Software	1382.5	95%	NA	99%	455	92%	NA	96%	568.2	96%
Books	128	NA	130	NA	130	NA	40	NA	40	NA
Totals	NA		1893.3		1933		1085.1		2137.7	

[1] 2002 Figures

Source: International Intellectual Property Alliance, 2004 Special 301: People's Republic of China.

Exhibit 5-1 Estimated Piracy Losses in China for Digitized Products, 1999-2003 (US$ Million).

Infringement of digitized and printable IPR in China includes the massive unlicensed use of movies and other contents by movie theatres, TV, and cable operators, both legitimate and pirate; unlicensed use of software both on the consumer and business side; and unauthorized production and distribution of various optical discs (CD-ROM, DVD, CD, and VCD). The capacity is certainly there: The International Intellectual Property Alliance (IIPA) estimates the disk production capacity on mainland China at 686 million. Add a Taiwan capacity of 990 million and Hong Kong with 1.94 billion (These three Greater China economies are numbers 1, 2, and 3 globally), and you have a production capacity of 3.5 billion discs. By comparison, capacity in number 4, Thailand, is estimated at 357 million, while India has a capacity of a mere 49 million. Not all the capacity is used illegally, but the IIPA estimates that 80 percent of Chinese producers make at least one pirated version. In 2003, the piracy rate for DVDs had reached 95 percent, the highest since 1996.

Operations have become increasingly sophisticated. For example, pirate syndicates now use machines that have been adjusted to produce discs minus their System Identification Number (SID) codes. The quality is often surprisingly good, and "time to market" has been cut drastically. A few years ago, low-quality pirated versions of newly released movies appeared within weeks of their official debut. Today, pirated DVD versions of new movies appear in Chinese streets within hours of their release, and often even before the official release. The bootlegged version of *Pearl Harbor* appeared in Hong Kong on May 28, 2000, weeks ahead of the June 21 premier. In Taiwan, the movie was available in mid May, a month before the official premier.[8] As a result, producers have lost even the short revenue-making window they previously had. In 2003, the U.S. motion picture industry grossed less than $3 million in a market estimated at $1.3–1.5 billion.

In software, China continues to occupy the upper ranks of software piracy. According to the Business Software Alliance, 92 percent of the software used in China in 2002 was pirated, placing it second behind Vietnam, which has a much smaller economy. The Chinese rate has moved little over the years, registering 97 percent in 1994 and 91 percent in 1999. By comparison, the Philippines reduced its piracy rate from 94 percent in 1994 to 68 percent in 2002; South Korea moved from 75 to 50 percent; and Bulgaria from 94 to 68 percent. In 2001, China was ranked third in terms of the overall losses for the software industry with losses of around $1.7 billion. Today, it is number one, with a loss count of $2.4 billion (2002 figures), 18 percent of the world total.

There are some bright spots, however. For instance, losses in journal piracy have been cut dramatically between 2001 and 2002. The good news also carries a dark side, however: The news suggests that the Chinese government is capable of getting a handle on the piracy problem when it wishes, which is where local interests are relatively minor and technology transfer is not part of the equation. The measures also lag behind the march of new technology, which continues to raise the enforcement bar. The proliferation of electronic publishing makes it easier to expropriate copyrights by simply downloading electronic journals using falsely obtained passwords.

The Enforcement Failure

By now, China has developed a comprehensive legal framework relating to IPR protection, which by and large complies with international standards and treaties such as the Berne Convention and the Trade Related Intellectual Property (TRIP) agreement. The framework still has many holes, however. China has not signed Internet-related provisions, and its laws permit the free use of copyright material, such as software, for "learning purposes." Government usage is also excluded under existing law. Narrow definitions (such as using seized material as a measure of scale of fake production), low trigger thresholds, and minor remedies (fines so small that they fail the economic test of deterrence) underlie the greatest problem—enforcement—whether administrative, criminal, or civil. Dr. Boam, the minister counselor, put it succinctly when he said that the IPR agreements signed by China may "have *reduced the growth* of the violations."

In 2002, 852 raids/searches relating to motion pictures were conducted by administrative authorities, with a conviction rate of 99.5 percent. Of those, 764 resulted in fines of less than $1,000, 43 resulted in a $1000–$5,000 fine, and only two resulted in a $5,000–10,000 fine.[9] Among the reasons for the low fines is that infringement is calculated in terms of the value of the pirated or counterfeit good rather than that of the original product, and warehousing falls short of proving intent to sell. It is no wonder that the Report to Congress on WTO Compliance concludes that "infringers consider the seizure and fines simply to be a cost of doing business."[10] The situation is even worse when it comes to criminal procedure, where the Report notes, "Criminal enforcement has virtually no deterrent effect on infringers." The criminal process has a threshold of 200,000 yuan (about $24,000) for firms and 50,000 (about $6,000) for individuals. Not only are these thresholds high to begin with, but they also are counted per seizure and not inventory amounts and are assessed in terms of bogus product value. As a result, few violators are brought to justice. According to the IIPA, in 2002, there were 80 raids relating to motion picture violations in Shanghai and Beijing, but only 3 cases resulted in actual prison terms. Finally, plaintiffs in civil process find a judiciary system that lacks independence and basic legal skills and usually have to carry the expenses incurred by investigators in addition to their own.

The Globalization of Piracy and Counterfeiting

The new frontier for the counterfeiting and piracy industry is the international arena. Bogus goods represent, per some estimates, close to 7 percent of global trade and are growing, incurring $300 billion in yearly losses to legitimate producers. Yamaha, for instance, estimates that every year, more than 100,000 China-made copies of its motorcycles find their way into overseas markets. Such exports require a sophisticated logistic and distribution network with global knowledge and reach. Would-be purveyors of pirated and counterfeit goods need to contend with legal systems that are much less tolerant about the practice than the Chinese authorities. They face the risk of seizure at the border or in land as well as criminal persecution and heavy punishment. What they do not need to worry about is the point of origin: The export of counterfeit and pirated goods does not constitute an actual sale according to Chinese law and hence is not considered a criminal offense. As confirmed by the WTO report to Congress, the Chinese Customs Service refuses to block exports of counterfeited goods even when presented with evidence. Once the fake goods leave the country, it becomes much more difficult to track them. Jack Clode, managing director of the Hong Kong Office of Kroll FactFinders, recalls a case of a counterfeit good produced in China with Taiwanese financing and shipped by a Hong Kong registered trading company to Brazil by way of India and Panama.[11]

On the demand side, developing country authorities often lack the ability and the will to crack down on counterfeit and pirated products. Some benefit from the trade by acting as principals or middlemen or are being paid to keep mum. In other instances, authorities see the flow as a way to keep a lid on domestic prices and have little sympathy for the plight of who they see as rich country multinationals using monopoly power. This is the case in much of Africa (especially where corruption is rampant, such as Nigeria) and in many parts of Asia (such as India, Pakistan, Malaysia, Indonesia, Myanmar), the Middle East (such as Saudi Arabia), Russia, and Latin America (such as Argentina and Brazil). Increasingly, however, fake goods find their ways into developed country markets. Chinese-made counterfeit Gillette razors and batteries, according to the company, are sold not only in South America and the former Soviet Union, but also in North America and Europe. In 2002, China was first on the list of U.S. customs seizures, with over $48 million worth of counterfeit goods apprehended in 1,488 seizures. Taiwan and Hong Kong ranked second and third. The EU reports that of the 95 million counterfeit goods seized in 2001, 18 percent were of mainland China origin. One can guess that for every product seized, many more make it into the market. The situation seems to be getting worse: The IIPA reports that the number of made-in-China counterfeit DVDs seized in the UK rose from 2,000 in the first quarter of 2003 to 77,000 in the second and third quarters. Operations are increasingly taking the appearance of a respectable business operation, where foreign buyers visit established showrooms and place orders for fake goods. Sellers offer increasingly diverse counterfeit brands and offer customization in terms of appearance, packaging, and labeling; and, as befit a full-service operation, buyers are offered shipping and custom avoidance logistics.

Fake inputs are not only exported from China. Bogus inputs are imported into the country from Vietnam, Malaysia, Taiwan, and Hong Kong, among others, for mainland assembly of both pirated/counterfeit and "legitimate" goods. Components unavailable from counterfeiters but vital for fake product assembly flow from developed country makers who do not care much, or have no idea, how their wares are being used. China is thus becoming the locus of a broad network that permits economies of scale and specialization, leveraging the competitive advantage of diverse locations the way a legitimate multinational would. The country is also becoming an electronic hub, its ISPs hosting infringing sites that allow for free downloading of music and other content.

A final and worrisome expression of the globalization of pirated and counterfeit products is the increasing involvement of international crime syndicates. The incentive is clear: *Time Europe* gives the example of a drug dealer who pays about $47,000 for a kilo (roughly 2.4 pounds) of cocaine and sells it for a street price of $94,000, pocketing about 100 percent in profit. Alternatively, the dealer can buy 1,500 pirated copies of Microsoft Office 2000 and pocket a 900 percent profit.[12] There are indications that these margins now attract the interest of international terror groups who view it as an effective way to fund their operations.

Going Forward

The optimistic scenario is for China to incrementally crack down on violators as a result of pressure exerted by industrialized countries, the continuous evolution of its legal system, and the realization that the current climate puts a damper on the prospects for developing indigenous industry in such areas as software. The avalanche of local outfits commandeering the images of China's manned space flight with its first "taikonaout" reminded the government that lack of intellectual property protection could come back to haunt it. Optimists also point to the establishment of IPR courts and amendments to the Copyright Law that signal intent to implement WTO commitments, as well as enhanced compliance in magazine publishing.

Pessimists need to look no further than the current statistics and the resilience of local authorities and their protégés. The pessimist scenario calls for expansion in the range, scope, and geographic reach of pirated and counterfeited industries brought about by the consolidation of production and distribution in major centers; technological advances that make piracy ever cheaper and easier; and the growing capabilities, resources, and cooperation among pirate enterprises. As Exhibit 5-2 shows, the pessimists, at least at the moment, appear to have the upper hand.

Industrial Category	Improved	Unchanged	Worse	Much Worse
Food manufacturing	14.29%	23.81%	40.47%	21.43%
Clothing, textiles, shoes	12.5%	18.75%	43.75%	25.0%
Daily-use products	0.0%	11.76%	41.18%	47.06%
Agricultural machinery	20.0%	0.0%	60.0%	20.0%
Transportation equipment	28.57%	0.0%	28.57%	42.86%
Ordinary machinery	0.0%	0.0%	31.35%	68.75%
Electric and electronics	13.04%	17.39%	39.13%	30.44%
Overall	9.79%	16.08%	42.66%	31.47%

Source: PRC State Council Research and Development Center, data cited in D.C.K. Chow, *A Primer on Foreign Investment Enterprises and Protection of Intellectual Property in China*. The Hague: Kluwer, 2002. Values shown are percentage of companies in each industrial category.

Exhibit 5-2 Expectations Regarding Improvement in China's Piracy Climate .

Navigating Pirate Seas

Piracy, counterfeiting, and other derivatives pose different challenges and produce a different repertoire of responses. For instance, it is easier to go after counterfeiters who try to pass a fake for an original in a home country court than it is to go after a pirate where a plaintiff will have to get into the lengthy and difficult process of proving that a product design infringes on its rights. Counterfeit products are also subject to seizure by custom and police authorities, which serves as an additional deterrent to the exportation of the product. This is not the case for products based on pirated design or processes. What the various phenomena have in common is that they undermine a key corporate asset, which often underpins the very competitiveness of a company and challenges it to come up with new strategic and operational responses.

Given the prevalence of the pessimistic view and the lack of incentive for the Chinese government—especially at the local level—to act against IPR infringement, firms will have to figure out how to compete in an environment where legal protections are lacking and where their technology and trademark assets are up for grab. Aside from building coalitions—such as the IIPA, the Global Business Leaders Alliance Against Counterfeiting, the International Anti Counterfeiting Coalition, and the Business Software Alliance—that lobby their governments to pressure the Chinese authorities and try to educate the public about the detriments of IPR infringement, it is up to the individual enterprise and the industry group to come up with the proper initiatives and defenses.

In some instances, IPR infringement may undercut the business model of a company. For instance, as Blockbuster found out, why would a consumer rent a video or DVD when he can buy a good-quality copy for less than the cost of the rental? This, in addition to high operating costs, was a major factor in Blockbuster's decision to exit the Hong Kong market.[13] Others have had to tinker with their business model to adjust for the infringement realities: Movie studios and publishers now opt for global releases, reducing the time available to pirates and counterfeiters to come up with a bootlegged version (although this does not help much when the pirated version is available prior to the official release).

Other firms are learning to protect their technology and know-how to the extent possible. For some, this means the development of a "smart chip" that assemblers cannot access or decipher. For others, the steps are as simple as stamping their logo on all component parts. Others rely on their ability to come up with new technology at a pace faster than imitation. Still others try to protect themselves by becoming "assemblers" who farm out production to Chinese contractors while maintaining core and overall knowledge at home. This strategy, too, is not full proof as it often underestimates Chinese informal networks, which serve as knowledge transfer conduits.

In and of itself, avoiding a Chinese presence does not prevent piracy and counterfeiting. As Boam notes, your starting point should be that "If it can be copied, it will." Physical presence makes it easier to imitate an intricate process—especially one that involves local suppliers who may then disseminate the knowledge. A foreign firm with Chinese operations may, however, do a better monitoring job and be in a better position to pressure the authorities to take action. Companies like Gillette increasingly take on the compliance burden and fund raids on their own. Those who decide to stay out of China are also missing on the opportunities in the Chinese market. Opting for a wholly owned subsidiary usually reduces the extent of technology leakage since cooperative ventures are effective vehicles for knowledge transfer, especially when the local partner has considerable learning capabilities.

Finally, as Boam points out, IPR protection should be part and parcel of the business plan of any company that intends to do business in China. This often implies taking a different approach to the one taken at home or in other foreign markets. Universal Music Group has recently announced a business model that is supposed to reduce its vulnerability to IPR violation. In cooperation with Shanghai Media Group, Universal will not only distribute its music but will diversify by developing local artists and use media, such as mobile phones, that can be monitored better.[14]

6

The Business Challenge

China's rise has already left its mark on businesses throughout the world. If you are in a labor-intensive industry, such as textiles, apparel, shoes, and man-made luggage, Chinese competition may have driven you out of business. If you occupy the higher end of the market, you may have gotten there as a defensive move against low-cost Chinese imports only to find out that this segment, too, is susceptible to competition from China and from other countries escaping the low margin zone. If you are a producer of durable household goods, such as appliances, you may still be in business courtesy of Chinese manufacturing or outsourcing; perhaps you are already not doing much more than slapping your brand label on a Made in China product. If you currently have no connection to China, you may be thinking of establishing one as you read these pages. As a supplier, you may be asking yourself whether you will be replaced by a Chinese competitor, and if you're a buyer, you may wonder if you should retain some of your domestic or third-country sources as a hedge against interruption in Chinese supplies.

The "first impact" of China's rise has been more apparent in some countries than in others (for example, more in the U.S., less in the European Union, or EU) and has been felt more in labor-intensive and low or intermediate technology areas than in technology-intensive areas. In the United States, China leads in such categories as footwear, toys, and household wooden furniture, among others, and, with the expiration of the Multifiber Arrangement and China's World Trade Organization (WTO) ascension, is about to take over textile and apparel. Three years earlier, when quotas on manmade fiber luggage were eliminated, unit price dropped by half and China's share of the global market rose fivefold. During the same period, U.S. luggage imports from Mexico declined by half, prompting the closing of several factories. Exports from Thailand and the Philippines also took a plunge.[1]

China's advance in the labor-intensive categories will not make many waves in the United States, which exited many such product lines long ago. For instance, a survey conducted by the American Rubber & Plastics Footwear Manufacturers Association (RPFMA) found that only 17 types or rubber/fabric and plastic/protective footwear, representing merely 5 percent of the footwear sold in the United States, are still produced here. The impact will be felt, however, in industrialized countries that have shielded their producers via a combination of subsidies and trade protection, and especially in developing nations that have relied on lower pay and proximity to market to stay the course. The travails of those developing economies will come back to haunt the industrialized nations who supply much of the value added in their production chain, provide aid to their struggling economies, and are host to their immigrants. As the radius of affected industries and product lines expands to cover a broader product array, industrialized nations will be further drawn into "the China debate" on its social and political ramifications.

In business, the rise of China will challenge basic assumptions regarding the nature of national and firm competitiveness, the value of geographic proximity, and the cost of market entry and exit. Location advantages that have underpinned company survival and prosperity for decades—and sometimes for centuries—will be questioned, and the global mobility of production factors will accelerate under a global supply chain. As on prior occasions of dramatic economic shift, the coming changes will test both external and internal alliances. Players will be playing by new rules, with new winners and losers created.

How should businesses prepare for the Chinese century? Preparation begins by understanding the nature of the coming change and assessing its impact on one's industry, firm, and individual employees. Preparation continues with a willingness to re-evaluate the very *raison-d'être* of the organization, questioning not only practices and routines but also the fundamental assumptions on which the business model rests. The re-evaluation will often call into question the adequacy of responses that have worked well in the past but may not hold this time. For instance, an opinion prepared for the Department of Commerce and the U.S. Trade Representative notes that the few leather tanneries that survived in the United States did so by focusing on the high-end automotive and furniture upholstery market; however, the Chinese move up-market is occurring at such a pace that this strategy is now called into question. As a whole, "business as usual" solutions will no longer work. Firms must rethink their entire value chain, which will likely lead to a new business model or to an outright exit.

Industry Tales

America's Clothier

In the 1840s, a British author wished, "If we could only persuade every person in China to lengthen his shirt-tail by a foot, we could keep the mills of Lancashire working around the clock.[2] Some 160 years later, this assessment of the Chinese impact on the textile and clothing trade is about to come true, except that the mills doing the overtime will not be in Lancashire or North Carolina but in Zhejiang and Jiangsu. As for the customers, they will be all over the globe. Between 1989 and 1999, China's share of the G-7 apparel market doubled, reaching 20 percent, according to OECD figures. China's clothing exports have continued to rise since 1999, passing the $70 billion mark in 2002. China is now the number one foreign source for the clothing sold in the U.S. Its 12 percent share is surely understated, because it does not count Hong Kong's 4-plus percent (which is at least partially mainland made) or the $160 million worth of smuggled clothing seized by U.S. Customs.[3] China, says the International Trade Commission (ITC), "is expected to become the 'supplier of choice' for most U.S. importers." The American Textile Manufacturers Institute (ATMI) estimates that by 2006, China will control more than 70 percent of the U.S. import market (see Exhibit 6-1). The Institute bases its predictions on 29 apparel categories, for which quotas were abolished on January 1, 2002, resulting in China's share of the American market rising from 9 percent in 2001 to 45 percent by the end of the first quarter of 2003. The only thing that might prevent China from cornering the entire market, according to the ITC and U.S. manufacturers and retailers, is the reluctance of buyers to be completely dependent on a single source.

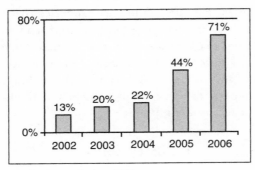

Source: The American Textile Manufacturers Institute, 2003.

Exhibit 6-1   China's Projected Control of the U.S. Textile and Apparel Import Market.

The U.S. market will not be the only one affected. World Bank forecasts that China will increase its share of the global clothing market, currently at roughly 17 percent, to 45 percent in the second half of the decade. A Chinese study estimates that as a result of WTO accession, China's apparel output will increase by almost 40 percent, while its textile output will grow by about 25 percent.[4] Chinese firms are gearing for the challenge. Data from the International Textile Manufacturers Federation shows that China accounts for 57.5 percent of all new shuttleless looms ordered during the 2000–2001 period. Further, 9.9 percent were ordered from Taiwan and Hong Kong. The U.S., the EU, and Canada *combined* account for 13.6 percent of the orders.

China's winning formula rests not only on low wages. As the ITC notes, China does not have the lowest wages in this sector, but it has the lowest per-unit costs due to higher productivity and scale economies. The country has the supporting industries that facilitate production; for instance, it is the largest manufacturer of man-made fibers. Vertical integration of large manufacturers permits rapid response and keeps outsiders away from the value chain. Chinese apparel makers are also better capitalized than developing country makers, permitting the introduction of the newest technology. The result is a one-stop shop unavailable anywhere else. China will become the supplier of choice, offers the ITC report, "because of its ability to make almost any type of textile and apparel product at any quality level at a competitive price." Where the Chinese still lack is in the creative aspects—in particular product design—but they can make up for that by knocking off foreign designs, a difficult thing to detect in any environment, let alone that of China.

China's advance will come at the expense of other industry players. An IMF report estimates that all other clothing exporters will suffer a significant drop, ranging from 14.4 percent for industrial nations, 32.2 for Latin America, and 32.4 for Africa.[5] The hardest hit will not be the developed nations who can redeploy their resources into sectors where they are more competitive and can obtain higher margins, but the developing and especially the least-developed economies that will be hard pressed to find alternative venues for growth and employment. ITC data shows that textile and apparel constitute 86 percent of Bangladesh's merchandise exports, 83 percent of Haiti's exports, and 63 percent of Honduras' exports. For Lesotho, in sub-Saharan Africa, the textile and apparel category accounts for 94 percent of all merchandise exports. The sub-Saharan region has already seen a dramatic decline in nightwear exports (a category where they compete with China in the U.S. market), from 98,000 dozens in 2001 to less than 30,000 in 2003. Lacking prospects for substitution, nations such as Lesotho are faced with grim prospects that will worsen an already bad economic situation, with political and social ramifications to come.

Even though developing economies will be on the firing line, developed countries will share the pain. Nations that have protected themselves from earlier entrants such as Taiwan and Korea by retrenching into the high-end, exclusive sides of the market will not be immune this time. ATMI projects losses of about $2.5 billion for EU exports to the U.S. Italy is forecasted to lose over $1.2 billion worth of exports in the American market, and even its top-of-the-line firms that have been in business for centuries are now threatened.[6] Canada is also projected to lose close to $2 billion of U.S.-destined apparel exports. Regions that are reliant on textile and apparel (such as North Carolina) will lose much of their domestic market, as well as the foreign markets they still dominate as exporters and as suppliers of fabric or yarn (such as the Caribbean). ATMI projects the closure of 1,300 U.S. textile plants in a three-year period—roughly a plant a day—although the enactment of the Central American Free Trade Agreement has served to stave off such a collapse for both U.S. and Central American firms. The United States and other rich nations will have to find a substitute for the lost export revenues of Haiti and Honduras. France will do the same for its former colonies in North and West Africa, extending regional interdependencies. Joining them will be a more assertive China, which will leverage its position to score political points with America's and the EU's closest neighbors by offering them bits and pieces in what will become a global supply chain whose "heart" (design, logistics, finance, and so on) resides in China.

Furniture from Afar

In 1993, imports represented about a quarter of the household wooden furniture sold in the United States; by 2002, they amounted to almost half. The difference can be easily accounted for: Between 1996 and 2002, U.S. imports of Chinese household furniture rose more than sixfold from $741 million to $4.8 billion. U.S. imports from China, by then the world's leading maker and exporter of wooden furniture, rose 75 percent between 2000 and 2002.[7] During the same period, production of all wooden furniture in the United States, including that made with imported components, declined from $12.12 billion to $10.67 billion.[8] The industry has been on a downward employment trend for years, having shed some 50 percent of its 150,000 strong workforce in the 1980s and 1990s, a result of automation and productivity improvements more than foreign competition. China's resurgence has greatly accelerated the pace, however, with the industry losing a further 28 percent (roughly 30,000 jobs) in just three years (2000–2002) according to the U.S. Department of Labor.

Edward M. Tashjian, vice president of marketing for Century Furniture of North Carolina, noted in a testimony before the House Committee on Small Business in June 2003 that a Chinese bedroom set comparable to his company's $22,755 offering was priced at $7,070, or 69 percent lower. Even if the quality of the Chinese product were lower (which is not necessarily the case), price advantage of that magnitude would be hard to pass over even by discerning consumers. The pressure on revenues and margins is evident: In a petition filed on October 31,

2003, a group of 28 U.S. furniture makers argued that between 2000 and 2002, sales by group members fell by 23 percent, and operating income declined by 75 percent. The petition stated, "It is no exaggeration to say that the imports from China have singlehandedly forced the industry into a tailspin so swift and so deep that it may soon become irreversible." The group accused their Chinese competitors of unfair pricing in the American market while benefiting from Chinese government subsidies and currency manipulation.

The U.S. industry, on its part, seems to have been caught unprepared. Dave Dyer, senior vice president of operations for Henredon Furniture Industries, Inc., told the Subcommittee on Commerce, Justice, State, and the Judiciary Appropriations House Committee on Appropriations on May 22, 2003, "Had someone suggested to me five years ago that we would be vulnerable to an onslaught of low-cost furniture products originating offshore, I would not have believed it." The common wisdom that the upper-end market was immune to low-cost competition was proven wrong as the Chinese manufacturers increasingly eyed the upper market on its fatter margins and sought to expand into other product categories. Tashjian projected that cheap imports—especially from China—would soon spread to upholstered products, such as sofas; Mr. Dyer observed that imports in the upholstery segment rose from $20.4 million in 1996 to $313 million in 2002, a fifteenfold increase. Local manufacturers in this segment were buffered in the past by the need for customization, but improved communications and logistics are bringing down the response time of Chinese makers—and with it the advantage of locally based production.

The wooden furniture tale reveals the depth of emotions that now surround the China debate ("Is God an American?" asked an importer of Chinese furniture[9]) and the difficulty of building an effective coalition to put obstacles in the way of Chinese imports. Major U.S. furniture retailers, many of whom import from China, offer little support for American manufacturers, and the major producers, like Missouri-based Furniture Brands and Virginia-based Hooker, are increasingly dependent on Chinese outsourcing and are reluctant to take a stand against imports.[10] In the political arena, the elected representatives of regions that are reliant on the furniture industry, such as North Carolina, find it difficult to solicit the support of their colleagues from Virginia, Mississippi, Ohio, Tennessee, New York, Indiana, Michigan, and

Illinois, where furniture manufacturing represents a smaller part of the economy, not to mention California and Oregon, which have negligible participation in the industry.

The Geography of the China Impact

China's business impact comes in many colors, from price pressures on domestic and third-market producers to competition for foreign investment dollars. Among industrialized nations, the United States has so far been the hardest hit: It takes the bulk of China's imports but has been relatively unsuccessful in exporting into China's burgeoning market. In the meantime, the EU and Japan are feeling the pressure of a rising China, which coincides with the internal restructuring of their economies. Nonetheless, China weighs more heavily on other developing nations, especially those who lack the resources and capabilities to redeploy into areas not threatened by Chinese competition. Some of those nations will view China's rise as an opportunity to engage in overdue reforms, whereas others will appeal to their developed brethren for help in the form of preferential trade agreements and outright handouts. The result may be even greater dependence on outside patrons (China including), with its attendant economic, political, and social correlates.

Holding Its Own: The European Union

While China dominates a number of product categories in the EU market (such as microwave ovens), Europe's deficit with the country is about one third that of the U.S.—not a lot for a bloc that as a whole maintains a trade surplus. According to Dr. Thomas Boam, minister counselor for commercial affairs at the U.S. Embassy in Ottawa, Canada, who formerly held the same position in the Beijing embassy, there are good reasons for the EU's superior trade performance in the China market.

First, Boam says, Europeans trust their governments and Non-Government Organizations (NGOs) more than Americans and utilize their help to reduce error rate. Second, Europeans heavily subsidize sales using a mixture of credits and outright gifts. (The Europeans assert that the U.S. provides its own subsidies.) Boam recalls the case of Cummins Diesel, which lost a bus engine deal to Iveco after the Italian firm came in with government subsidies that amounted to 70% of the purchase price. U.S firms lack access to subsidized credits such as U.S. AID, which has been on hold since the Tiananmen massacre. Third, European firms are conscious of exports, while America's smaller enterprises see the international market as a temporary stop gap to help ride domestic downturns. Fourth, European firms have no qualms about paying bribes (Europeans differ, but until recently, bribe paying abroad was legal—even tax deductible—under the laws of Germany, for instance).

Fifth, European political leaders intervene on behalf of their firms, while U.S. political leaders bash China on human rights. "Our leaders may be right, but the Europeans get the contracts," notes Boam. Sixth, American firms are burdened by the U.S. superpower status. Chinese officials worry about the U.S. imposing sanctions to make a political point and hence will buy U.S. equipment but not systems; however, they know that the Europeans "will have nothing stand in the way of a deal." Seventh, the Europeans protect their domestic markets from Chinese imports, but the U.S. does not. Finally, because of the U.S. deficit, the Chinese have huge reserves of U.S. dollars that they are unable to spend in the U.S., so it goes toward buying Japanese and European goods. In other words, the Chinese have the capacity to balance their trade with Europe because of the U.S. trade deficit.

There are a couple of other explanations: The EU has Eastern Europe as a lower-cost base in its own backyard; the U.S. has Mexico, but that environment does not offer the same advantages. European markets are more closed and fragmented, making it more difficult for China's newcomer firms to penetrate the market. Structural rigidities in the EU increase the cost of shutting down operations and moving them offshore. Finally, Europe does not have the U.S. cold war "baggage" and friction surrounding sensitive issues such as visa issuance. The EU has also been less restrictive in terms of technology transfer, although this may come back to haunt it as Chinese recipients become direct competitors. So far, the EU has tried to act in tandem regarding China affairs, but this masks the divergent interests of those members that have a substantial trade deficit with China (such as the United Kingdom and the Netherlands) vis-à-vis those who have only a small deficit (such as Germany).

The Invasion of Japan

In the Japanese market, the impact of a rising China was held back by price insensitivity, high brand consciousness, and a fragmented, multilayered, and nepotistic retail and distribution network. With the introduction of fundamental changes in the Japanese business and retail environment (such as the growth of large discounters) and the rising cost pressures of a deflationary economy, Chinese products have started to penetrate the market. The first wave was led by Made in China Japanese name brands such as National/Panasonic (brand names of Matsushita Corporation) and Toshiba, but Japanese consumers can now find Haier appliances and other branded Chinese goods priced substantially lower than domestic makes. Apparel imports have risen by half over the past five years and are projected to continue their expansion. China is now the largest exporter of goods to Japan, having surpassed the United States, which held the lead for half a century. Chinese imports have been blamed for Japanese deflation (in fairness, they were at most a contributing factor, and, possibly even a driver of market demand) and for "hollowing out" Japan's manufacturing core, a criticism that is now echoed in the United States.

Some Japanese firms were caught off guard. Sanyo's appliance division, for instance, is suffering serious losses. Others have been busy moving operations to China, where they find what they lack in Japan: low wages and benefits (whereas the aging Japanese society forces ever-growing pension contributions), a stable currency (the yen is appreciating), and reasonable real estate costs (for manufacturing sites). China also provides Japanese manufacturers with the opportunity to build state-of-the-art facilities unencumbered by obsolete design and outdated machinery, serve a high-growth market, and tap a future innovation source. Japanese firms have come to the realization that China can be a vital part in their bid to remain competitive. They are preparing for the Chinese century by sharpening R&D competencies and building the supply chain necessary for China-based manufacturing, including a new international airport near Nagoya that will handle mostly China flights.

Mexico Undone

For years, Mexico enjoyed a double advantage over its developing country competitors vying to serve the U.S. market: geographical proximity and NAFTA-generated tariff-free access. The value of proximity has gradually eroded (although it remains vital for certain product lines). Ricardo Haneine, director of the A.T. Kearny Mexican office, calculated that proximity yields no more than five cents on the dollar for Mexican manufacturers compared to their Chinese competitors.[11] In some categories, such as apparel, where Mexico competes with China head on, operations are located deep in the Mexican hinterland, lowering proximity advantages. And, with China about to enjoy much-improved access to the U.S. market, the NAFTA advantage is dissipating as well. Mexico remains competitive in areas such as automotive, where proximity and close integration are especially important and where local facilities have made strides in quality and productivity, and in computer equipment, where labor represents a relatively modest portion of product cost. Mexico is losing ground, however, in telephone equipment, household appliances, and electrical assemblies, such as transformers.[12] The result has been disturbing: Between 1980–1999, according to IMF data, Mexico racked up an export gain of $121 billion compared to China's $177 billion; in the 1999–2002 period, China's gain edged up to $188 billion, while Mexico's plunged to a mere $13 billion.[13]

In textile and apparel, which account for 6 percent of Mexico's merchandise exports, the impact has been devastating. For years, Mexican garment exports rose in tandem with those of China. In 1978, Mexico had a 0.6 percent share of the global market in clothing and textile; by 1999, the share rose to 4.5 percent. During the same time period, China's share rose from 2.4 to 15.4 percent.[14] As recently as 2000, per Department of Commerce figures, the U.S. volume of textile and apparel imports from Mexico was more than double that from China, but by 2002, the Chinese were in the lead. In the categories where China competes directly with Mexico, such as integrated products, the growth was more than threefold just from 2001 to 2002, according to the ITC. It is going to get worse: According to ATMI, the U.S. market share of brassieres made in Mexico is projected to fall from 47 percent in 2001 to 6 percent in 2004; China's share is expected to rise from 5 to 67 percent. According to the *Wall Street Journal*, 325 of the 1,122 clothing maquiladoras have closed down since January 2001.[15] All in all, projects ATMI, Mexico's clothing industry will lose $5.4 billion as a direct result of China's entry. An ITC investigation notes that U.S. apparel companies and retailers have already reduced their sourcing in the country, and more plan to do so when the quota regime expires. Interviewees cited rising labor costs, inconsistent quality, low reliability, intratransit merchandise loss, limited availability of full-package service, and the inability of suppliers to diversify into fashion denim jeans, a higher margin product.

According to U.S. Census Bureau figures, in August 2002, overall U.S. imports from China surpassed those from Mexico for the first time ever. The two countries then alternated for several months as America's second and third largest import sources (after Canada), but by May 2003, China pulled away and did not look back. While the numbers for Mexico may temporarily rebound to reflect higher oil prices, the overall trend is unlikely to reverse. This does not mean that all of Mexico's troubles are China's fault. The country's dependence on the U.S. market means that its economic fate is closely tied to the ups and downs of the American economy. For instance, the bulk of the decline in Mexico's U.S.-destined machinery exports in 2001 can be explained by the 10 percent decline in the output of the American motor vehicle industry that year, which reduced its purchases of Mexican wiring harnesses by the same ratio. The same is true for household appliances, where U.S. imports from both China and Mexico have been on the increase.[16]

Other problems are of Mexico's own making but have been exposed in the glare of competition. Cofose, a Mexican organization for foreign trade promotion, organized a trip to China to compare the national competitiveness of the two locales. The Mexican visitors found China to be superior on all counts: China had, they observed, stronger national vision, sound long-term planning, a more favorable investment climate (clear regulations, tax incentives, order, and security), cheaper but more productive labor, and a lower raw material cost.[17] A GE study offers a more positive assessment, noting that while Mexico ranks lower than China on labor costs, electricity costs, and a supplier base, it does better (not surprisingly) on transportation costs and free trade agreements, but also on productivity, international telecommunications cost, technology transfer requirements, intellectual property rights (IPR) protection, management flexibility, and regulatory transparency.[18] The Mexican government has taken measures to lower the cost of manufacturing, reducing corporate taxes and offering cheap land and other subsidies, but it remains to be seen whether this will be enough to stop the tide of firms relocating to China and whether Mexican companies will be able to leverage China as a market or as a complementary producer.

Friends and Foes: ASEAN and Beyond

Most members of the Association of Southeast Asian Nations (ASEAN) have a trade surplus with China, supplying anything from food to raw materials and intermediate inputs. China, at the same time, has been encroaching on ASEAN's traditional territory of electronic assembly: As China's share of the global electronics market went up from 9.5 percent in 1992 to 21.8 percent in 1999, Singapore's share declined from 21.8 to 13.4. As China's personal computer production expanded from 4 percent of global output in 1996 to 21 percent in 2000, ASEAN's share dropped from 17 to 6 percent.[19] The ASEAN trade surplus has so far cushioned the pressure, but it is not clear it will be maintained. China's WTO accession is widely viewed as providing more opportunities to the developed nations that negotiated concessions for their favorite concerns (such as services for the United States) than to developing nations. ASEAN nations that provide intermediary inputs to China's rapidly expanding industry will fare better than developing countries in Latin America and Africa who are dependent on the labor-intensive sector that China now dominates. As China progresses, it will have a lesser need to import mid-technology components for which Chinese producers are emerging. In the meantime, ASEAN firms that are pushed out from lucrative end-product markets in the industrialized nations will lose not only revenues but also the learning and reputation that come with such presence. They will be increasingly dependent on China—a dependence they are already seeking to reduce by establishing alliances with other nations and by retaining alternative supply sources.

Beyond ASEAN, countries in Latin America, the Indian subcontinent, Eastern Europe and the former Soviet Republics, Africa, the Middle East, and Central Asia are importing large amounts of Chinese products. Some can offer something in return—in particular, oil and minerals for the growing Chinese economy (such as Russia and the Middle East) or, in some instances, technology (such as Israel and India). As the IMF report suggests, commodity imports explain China's high and balanced trade with many of "the 48 club"—the world's least developed economies. Less developed nations with no tradable commodities that the Chinese desire will have little to offer except perhaps a UN vote; they will, however, help China reposition itself as a Third World champion at the same time it seeks to attain a superpower status.

What's Coming

As Exhibit 6-2 shows, the Chinese industry has been moving from primary goods and basic manufactures toward the more sophisticated segments of the manufacturing sector. In 2002, according to the Chinese Ministry of Commerce, electronics and machinery constituted about half of the country's total export. China's share of the global electronic market has more than doubled in a decade and now exceeds 20 percent. Its share of the personal computer market has quintupled in five years. Most of the TV sets, video recorders, DVD players, and cell phones today are either made in China or include Chinese components. China's cost advantage is increasingly associated with high productivity, scale economies, supporting industries, and advanced manufacturing technologies rather than merely with low wages.

In the automotive industry, China is fast becoming an outsourcing hub for components, and it's emerging as a viable exporter. Volkswagen (VW) has already begun to export its China-made cars and is projecting substantial volume increases in the coming years. Honda has built the first export-only plant and is getting ready to start operations. Once the Chinese automotive market slows its rapid growth (admittedly years from now), the pressure to export will rise as manufacturers—both foreign firms and "national champions"—worry about utilizing the enormous capacity they have built up. Given the general overcapacity in the industry and the technological edge of the newer China plants, it is difficult to see how automotive manufacturing in developed markets such as the United States and Europe will not be affected.

A new crop of national champions leads China's charge in the technology-intensive sector. TCL is completing a merger with a unit of French Thomson that will make it the world's largest TV manufacturer. Haier has 6 percent of the global refrigerator market and manufactures also in the United States; Haier's competitor, Kelon, is not far behind. Lenovo (formerly Legend) in computers, servers, and cell phones (and increasingly in services); Huawei Technologies in telecommunications; China Netcom in phone service; and Pearl River in pianos are taking first steps in building global brands. Having endured stiff competition at home from both domestic and foreign players (most Chinese industries have low concentration rates, meaning the leading manufacturers control only a small share of the market), those firms have built competitive capabilities, among them the ability to respond

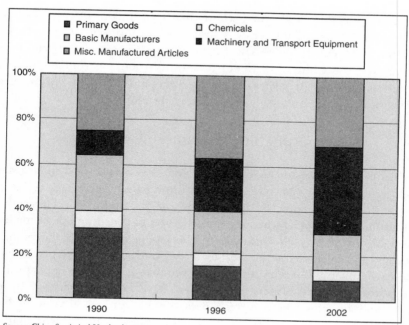

Source: China Statistical Yearbook, 2003.

Exhibit 6-2 Composition of China's Exports.

quickly to changing demand. Firms that have worked as Original Equipment Manufacturers (OEMs) or part suppliers to Western companies have learned the importance of shaving another minute from a production process or another cent in material cost. What they lack in technology, marketing, and logistic capabilities they make up by hiring staff—mostly locals who have worked previously for foreign multinationals—but also returnees and expatriates. They are also on the lookout for cross-border acquisition opportunities. Two Chinese firms, one of them completely lacking automotive technology, have been the frontrunners to purchase Sanyong Motors, a unit of the Korean chaebol, which will give the buyer immediate access to advanced technology and a global supply chain.

These developments will further increase the radius of China's influence. China's emerging national champions, already battling established multinationals in their home market, have their eyes set on international markets. Within a few years, Chinese consumer product maker (such as Nice, which outsells Unilever and P&G in the detergent category locally) will start their overseas push, opening a new competitive front. And while Chinese service providers are decades behind, they can leverage the financial capabilities of Taiwan, Hong Kong, and the Chinese Diaspora to solidify their position in shipping (where China is already a major player) and aviation, engineering services, and down the road, research and development.

Preparing for the Chinese Century

Business reaction to the China challenge has been mixed so far. Many industries and firms have been caught unprepared, failing to realize the threat to their current business model or the sudden acceleration of structural shifts that in the past took decades to consummate. Some have been blindsided by the promise of the China market to the point of neglecting the challenge in their own backyard; others have given up all too easily on the burgeoning Chinese economy, forfeiting opportunities to more aggressive players. Still others have been sidetracked by the tired and by now obsolete responses of U.S. unions that have been focusing on China's admittedly dismal human rights record while failing to offer much in a way of solutions besides veiled protectionism.

Some industry groups pin their hopes on political pressure, buoyed by the interest politicians have taken of late in the job issue, but they will be, at best, buying time. (Textile and apparel makers have already won some quota relief, but as safeguards expire at the end of 2008, this tactic, too, will have been exhausted.) Others believe that currency adjustment will take care of the problem, but they need to look no further than the mid 1980s, when the appreciation of the yen in the aftermath of the Plaza accord brought, at best, a temporary halt in the *growth* of the deficit. Even under a radical scenario of a 30–40% increase in the value of the yuan, China's labor-intensive products would continue to enjoy an enormous price advantage, although some categories, such as chip making, may see a difference. In short, businesses should not count on the government to bail them out but prepare for the new reality that is about to dawn.

A New Game Plan

For firms that operate in labor-intensive industries, the writing is on the wall. For many developed country firms, especially those lacking the pricing power of brand or specialized capabilities, the best option is simply to exit the market. This is a harsh remedy with ominous consequences for employees and communities, but one that may be preferable to slow bleeding because it avails capital and human resources to be redeployed rather than exhausted. Developing country firms stand a better chance because the improvements they need to make in the labor-intensive sector are more modest than those demanded of industrialized country competitors, but they still need to obtain the necessary know-how. Indeed, an alliance between a developed nation manufacturer with the requisite technology and process and a third country producer with a lower cost base is one way to meet the China challenge.

If a business does not wish to exit, it had better come up with a new game plan showing how it is planning to avoid being the "plant of the day" closure. It might want to explore product lines where it has specialized capabilities and labor constitutes a relatively minor part of total cost. In and of itself, automation may not do the trick. The Chinese are automating, too, when it makes sense, and their labor cost advantage may often compensate for lower automation. In a high-cost environment, reaching the point where productivity improvements outweigh wage cost advantage requires a high magnitude change, like that achieved by American Axle, which reduced the number of hours it needed to generate $1,000 in revenue from 10 in 1994 to 3.8 in 2003, while enhancing quality.[20]

One solution is to extend technological capabilities into related areas not only in manufacturing but also in higher growth services. SRC Holdings, for one, diversified into the higher margin areas of logistics and commercial software, publishing, banking, and the spa business to support its core manufacturing operations. Malden Industries went as far as utilizing some of its land in Lawrence, Massachusetts for real estate development while counting on research and technological advance to hold its own against Chinese competitors.[21] Customization, a traditional survival tool for many U.S. small and mid-size enterprises, can be a viable strategy where the product in question is small-batch, expensive, or difficult to transport, or requires lead time that is shorter than the Chinese production and shipping (typically three weeks) cycle.

In and of itself, moving up-market no longer ensures survival. As Henredon Industries found, Chinese firms are encroaching on this segment, joined by competitors from other countries, all trying to escape the same low margin fate. Branding is a critical component in this strategy, but with more developed country manufacturers exiting the market, Chinese firms have been able to buy established brand names, thus nullifying the effect. This leaves technological development and innovation, China's Achilles' heel, as a solution—as long as a company is in a position to protect it. A company's starting point should be that its technology and know-how are vulnerable, whether it has a China presence or not; as Boam says, "If it can be copied, it will." Being physically present in China will expose a company's production process on all its intricacies, but it will have more leverage with the Chinese authorities to crack down on violators, among other advantages. There are certain obvious steps a company can take to reduce the risk, from technological solutions (such as using a smart chip) to operational procedures (a company should think like an intelligence organization, sharing technology and know-how only to the extent necessary) and governance (a company should opt for a wholly owned foreign subsidiary, except where a Chinese partner can make vital and exclusive contributions unavailable from anyone else, and, when it has firm grounds to believe that the partner is unlikely to either copy the company's technology or forward it to a third party).

If You Can't Beat Them

With cost pressures likely to intensify in all but the most exclusive segments of the market, outsourcing can be a vital ingredient in a company's survival plan. Furniture Brands, the largest residential furniture company in the U.S., closed down 17 U.S. plants as part of a move to shift production to China. Henredon Furniture sources almost a third of its product line in low-cost economies, including China. GE is planning to do the same with its refrigerator line, while Maytag is importing Chinese components to lower the price of its dishwashers. Outsourcing permits the lowering of costs without sacrificing market presence and, with proper quality control, brand image. The strategy also has drawbacks, however, among them the grooming of future competitors, which can be offset partially by retaining core capabilities. Some firms, like Cutting Edge, a small Ohio division of CB Manufacturing, try to leverage their China outsourcing capabilities by offering third-party outsourcing services to small and mid-size firms.[22]

Outsourcing may not always be enough, even when accompanied by other measures. The *Wall Street Journal* reported the struggle of a remaining Furniture Brands plant in North Carolina to stay afloat by improving productivity, adjusting layout, tuning in to employee suggestions, and using some Chinese input, yet it is not clear that this will stave off eventual closure.[23] Or, take the case of Ohio-based Nippert, a tertiary supplier of copper rod and wire to the U.S. auto industry that came under intense pressure to cut costs by as much as 5 percent annually to compete with foreign sources. Having to meet requirements for ISO (International Organization for Standardization) certification and pollution control that its Asian competitors did not have to worry about and with no control over metal pricing (a major cost component), Nippert squeezed whatever efficiencies it could and then started outsourcing in Taiwan, saving as much as 70 percent in tooling costs. Yet, Chinese competition continued to erode its customer base. Faced with the loss of its biggest customer, who could no longer compete with a competitor who had moved production to China earlier, Nippert sold off its assembly business to focus on its core competency: the manufacture of copper shapes. (Final assembly is now in China.) With China cornering the market for scrap metal, prices for domestic producers rose, further weakening its position. The company started to shed staff, quality suffered, and with less capital available for R&D and equipment upgrades, chances for a rebound dimmed.[24]

While China's rise accelerates the plight of manufacturers like Nippert, it also opens new doors. China's outsourcing is not only a strategy for survival in a cutthroat business, but it's also an unprecedented opportunity for new entrants. Take the case of Dan Zubic, recently covered in the *Wall Street Journal*. An American who was laid off from his job at NEC's television making division, Dan contracted with one of the Taiwanese TV manufacturers (most of whom manufacture on the mainland) to form a new company,[25] something that could not even have been contemplated when GE, RCA, Motorola, and later Sony, Matsushita, and Samsung ruled the market.

Finally, China's almost balanced trade flow proves that it is not impossible to sell in that market, the fastest growing in the world. With many of the world largest companies, such as Goodyear, Toshiba, and Nestlé, expanding their China operations, they will be looking for partners and suppliers with whom they can work globally. If a company will not consider this option of servicing the Chinese market, another supplier—possibly from China—will. Success is by no means assured. To cite Dr. Boam, "There are only two kinds of foreign companies in China:

those that are making huge amounts of money and those that are losing their shirts. The latter group is not only sizable, but growing." To be counted among the first group, a company must do its homework, understand how the Chinese environment works, and determine how to develop and protect a competitive advantage under different game rules. The same formula applies to the China game as a whole.

7

East, East, and Away: Where the Jobs Are

The migration of jobs to foreign destinations, China included, has become a hotly debated topic in the United States and in other nations, mostly—but not only—in the industrialized world. Job migration has been blamed for a "jobless recovery" in America, with new job creation lagging behind economic recovery further than at any time since the aftermath of World War II, as well as for stalled employment growth in Mexico and in other developing economies. In fairness, job migration is not the only or even primary factor behind job losses: Productivity gains induced by technology (for example, automation), capital investment, process improvements, and enhanced skills; cyclical and nontrade related structural shifts; alternate employment in the service sector; and regulatory and tax burden are among the factors that influence the employment picture. Still, job migration in its various forms accounts for a significant portion of job losses in the U.S., as well as in other economies, and its impact will continue to loom large in the years to come.

Based on Trade Adjustment Assistance (TAA) data, 6.4 million American jobs were lost to foreign competition between 1979 and 1990—or, approximately one-third of the 17 million manufacturing jobs lost during that period, according to Lori Kletzer, a University of California–Santa Cruz economist.[1] Analyzing Department of Labor data, Bardhan and Kroll found that between 2001 and 2003, the U.S. manufacturing sector suffered a 12.8 percent decline in employment (versus a 1.4 percent addition in the service sector), but industries at risk of outsourcing experienced a steeper decline, with computer and electronic products and semiconductor and electronic components (sectors in which Chinese imports are prominent) falling at 24 and 22.9 percent below their prior staffing levels, respectively.[2] Goldman Sachs and Company estimates that 20 percent of U.S. manufacturing employment, representing one-half a million jobs and including those involving sophisticated design and technology, have moved overseas.[3]

China is not solely responsible for jobs lost to foreign competition, and—in the service sector—it is not even the primary culprit. If you are an information technology or call center worker, India would place higher than China. If you are an insurance claim processor, Irish workers may have already replaced you, only to face their own competition in the form of Polish recruits. If you are an aircraft designer, Russian replacements may be more of a concern. China is not yet a major player in services although it is already a destination for embedded software and for financial firm back-office business processes and application development, and a competitor in call centers for Japanese and Korean firms.[4] Figures compiled by McKinsey Global Institute show China to be a destination for only $1.1 billion in services versus $7.7 billion destined for India and $8.3 billion destined for Ireland (though the Chinese figures are still higher than those for Australia and Russia, among others).[5]

If you are in manufacturing, however, or are in one of the many sectors that support it directly (such as product design) and indirectly (such as engineering and consulting services), a 750 million strong Chinese workforce is not something you would want to discount in a global economy where production factors are ever more mobile. Historically more susceptible to employment shifts (for example, productivity in industry has risen much faster than in services), manufacturing has shed close to three million jobs in the U.S. in a mere three-year period. Many of those losses have little to do with foreign competition or are in sectors where employment has been declining for years. Nevertheless, job losses attributed to developing economies in general, and to China in particular, have stirred political backlash in the U.S., the European Union (EU), and Japan. China has also been blamed for job losses in developing economies like Mexico, which holds China responsible for fleeing foreign investors and for the country's shrinking share in lucrative export markets.

Job Migration: Myth and Fact

The vocabulary surrounding job migration can get confusing. Briefly, outsourcing is the farming out of portions of a company's value chain (such as an appliance motor) to other companies, divisions, or affiliates. Foreign outsourcing, or off-shoring (a term that may not only acquire virtual connotation but also involve the physical movement of value chain elements), is similar to outsourcing except that the work is farmed out overseas. Trade displacement is job loss due to foreign imports driving domestic producers out of the market. Trade displacement is defined and measured in terms of import competition in a focal market, but domestic workers also lose when the foreign markets to which they export shrink; additionally, they miss out on future demand at home and abroad. Outward foreign investment, another source of job loss, is when domestic manufacturers shift production to an overseas location or when a new plant is placed abroad and home country employees are not hired as a result.

There are no overarching statistics for job migration. The numbers that appear in the media typically refer only to one type of migration, (such as off-shoring or trade displacement, a usage which tends to discount the overall impact of job migration). For example, foreign outsourcing proponents point out that the phenomenon represents a very small portion of overall job loss, but rarely mention that it is only one aspect of foreign competition for jobs. In addition, some of the oft-cited estimates entail a clear downward bias. For instance, TAA statistics are based on the U.S. government program by that name, which, as Jon Honeck of Policy Matters Ohio notes, greatly undercounts job losses— to be counted, you must apply, but many workers are unaware of the program's existence and TAA does not cover service providers (even when related to manufacturing), (upstream or downstream) suppliers, or (until recently) jobs relocated to any country other than Mexico or

Canada.[6] As to outward foreign investment, because its impact is difficult to gauge, it is almost never included in job loss estimates; in contrast, inward investment often is, which amplifies the under-counting. The confusion surrounding the numbers makes them ripe for political hijacking by proponents, opponents, and other job migration constituencies.

Job Migration and Job Losses

What it clear is that the production flows underlying the various forms of job migration are on the rise. For instance, from 1987 to 1997, the share of foreign inputs in American manufacturing (an outsourcing measure) rose from 10.5 to 16.2 percent and in American high tech rose from 26 to 38 percent.[7] There is a general consensus that the U.S. is the leader in off-shoring with more than two-thirds of the global market, and that the flow will only grow; a recent survey of financial officers of U.S. firms found that 27 percent planned foreign outsourcing while 61 percent of those already engaged in the activity planned to expand outsourcing activities. In 2004, 86 percent of the companies DiamondCluster International polled expected to increase foreign technology outsourcing, compared to 32 percent just two years earlier.

Given the above trends, the job impact cannot be far behind; Forrester Research projects that by 2015, off-shoring will have generated a loss of 3.3 million U.S. jobs, especially in the service sector, representing more than $130 billion in wages (keep in mind that most of the impact is projected to occur in later years and that the yearly loss seems minute in a work force of 150 million). McKinsey Global Institute sees a loss of about 200,000 jobs a year through off-shoring, while Economy.com projects that the 300,000 jobs currently lost every year will double by the end of the decade.[8] By 2010, 277,000 jobs in computer science, 162,000 in business operations, and 83,000 in architecture will have moved from the U.S. to low wage countries like India and China.[9] Trade displacement—somewhat forgotten in the uproar surrounding off-shoring—continues to be a significant contributor to employment losses, averaging 270,000 jobs annually between 1989 and 2000 according to the Department of Labor Statistics.[10] A study by Policy Matters Ohio calculated that U.S. trade deficits between 1994 and 2000 removed 135,000 actual and potential jobs in Ohio alone, 100,000 of which where in the manufacturing sector. Finally, the U.S. has the largest outstanding stock of foreign direct investment, and its foreign affiliates—like those of other nations—compete with domestic jobs twice: first, by shifting company employment that would have taken place domestically; second, by exporting back to the U.S. market thereby displacing American workers employed by their domestic competitors.[11]

In Context

To put things in context, economies shed and create numerous jobs regardless of trade; this is especially true of the American economy that is more flexible than most others. Every year, millions of Americans separate from their workplace—voluntarily or otherwise—and millions of jobs are lost (many, like those of typists, never return) while millions of new jobs are created in a so-called "creative destruction" process. Job migration itself is not a one-way street; one country's outsourcing is another country's insourcing. The U.S. runs a huge deficit in merchandise trade, which destroys jobs via trade displacement but enjoys a considerable surplus in commercial services—a form of insourcing for the American economy—such as consulting or engineering services. The Institute for International Investment claims that, over the last fifteen years, insourced jobs have grown by an annual rate of 7.8 percent while outsourced jobs have grown at a rate of 3.8 percent. In 2001, according to Department of Commerce figures, U.S. companies exported $280 billion worth of services directly and $432 billion more through their affiliates; at the same time, foreign companies sold to the U.S. services in the amounts of $202 and $367 billion, respectively. U.S. exports of private services such as consulting, banking, and engineering exceeded $130 billion in 2003 while imports were lower at about $78 billion.[12]

Although outsourcing eliminates many jobs, it also creates employment. It does so directly by creating demand for employment in sectors associated with the mobility of production inputs and finished goods (such as logistics, shipping and retail) and indirectly by enhancing the competitiveness of the focal firm. Outsourcing permits a company to focus on what it does best (for example, designing and developing new products) and allows for the deployment of resources into areas of comparative advantage that, at least in developed economies, produce more value added and better paying jobs. President Bush's chief economic advisor was alluding to those benefits when he suggested that outsourcing was good for the U.S. economy, though he neglected to consider its downside potential or show sympathy for the workers displaced. In addition, workers in outsourcing destinations are often more motivated to do jobs viewed by those in an industrialized nation as less attractive.[13] Global Insight, a consultancy, argues that off-shoring lowers inflation and interest rates and raises productivity. According to Global Insight, off-shoring added a net of 90,000 jobs by the end of 2003 and will yield more than 300,000 jobs by the end of 2008 by making U.S. producers better competitors and exporters.

Imports need not result in job losses if the foreign producer decides to manufacture in the host market. While the U.S. has the largest foreign investment stock, it is also the primary destination for inward investment and was the second ranked recipient (following China) in 2003. Close to 6.5 million Americans are employed by the affiliates of foreign companies in the U.S. and, as the Organization for International Investment notes, foreign firms tend to pay more—on average—than their U.S. counterparts. Also, without imports, there would be no exports, which typically provide better than average compensation. Still, exports tend to create jobs while imports tend to destroy them, and the problem for the U.S. is that it runs an enormous trade deficit; in other words, the downside employment potential of imports outweighs the upside employment potential of exports.

Economic models such as that of the Economic Policy Institute (EPI), which capture the employment impact of both imports and exports, show a loss of three million U.S. jobs and job opportunities between 1994 and 2000—the difference between 2.77 million jobs created through exports and 5.8 million lost via imports.[14] Additionally, the jobs gained are not necessarily better than the jobs lost. Past wisdom was that the U.S. exported simple, low-paying jobs and imported high-skilled jobs. No more. Knowledge intensive jobs are now on the line. Finally, the people who lose jobs and those who gain jobs as a result of job migration are not the same people, do not work in the same industries, and do not live in the same regions. Thus, even if job migration were beneficial at the macro level, there remains the problem of those who pay the price for the supposedly common good.

Who Benefits?

The McKinsey Global Institute argues that off-shoring creates net additional value for the exporting economy. According to the McKinsey analysis (using off-shoring to India as an example), for every dollar off-shored, the U.S. economy accrues between $1.12 and $1.14 while the receiving country captures just 33 cents. The U.S. benefit comes from a combination of reduced costs (58 cents), purchases from U.S. providers (5 cents), and repatriated earnings (4 cents) for a current and directly retained benefit of 67 cents; an additional 45 to 47 cents is supposed to come from the redeployment of labor into higher value-added (and better-paying) jobs.

Since the McKinsey report does not provide the actual analysis on which the final numbers are based (McKinsey states that they are based on a conservative interpretation of historical patterns), it is impossible to pass judgment on their validity. Nonetheless, the report seems to make a number of optimistic assumptions that may not materialize. For instance, the profit repatriation component in the formula is suspect not only because foreign investment contracts in developing economies often limit profit repatriation but also because companies increasingly choose to retain earnings in higher growth markets such as China and India in order to fund further expansion. The McKinsey analysis also fails to capture the value of the capabilities that the receiving countries obtain as a result of outsourcing and that will eventually enhance their ability to compete with the origin-country producers. This benefit to the receiving country (which will eventually show up as trade displacement) challenges the largest benefit for the origin country, namely savings accrued to U.S. investors and/or consumers. McKinsey's calculation does not take into account the losses associated with loss of purchasing power by laid off workers (including loss of tax revenues), possibly because the assumption is that the gap will be more than made up by higher-paying jobs. It is not clear that this compensation will happen. And, if foreign producers end up in an oligopoly position (quite possible, given China's dominance in some product lines and ongoing consolidation of its industry), the savings to consumers may disappear. Finally, if indeed most benefits are accrued to investors and customers while most costs are born by employees, there might be a substantial social cost that is not factored into the McKinsey formula.

Macro Promise, Micro Reality

If—like the chairman of the Federal Reserve—you have an unfailing faith in the vibrancy of the U.S. economy, you are still left wondering about the prospects for your industry, firm, and job. The redeployment of resources that may be beneficial in the long run to the public at large presents immediate challenges to certain industries and job categories and—as a result—to individuals, families, and communities. Those affected will find little comfort in a common benefit that will not be shared by all or in the fact that (according to demographers' predictions) the U.S. will eventually be facing a shortage of employees as its population, like that of other industrialized countries, ages. Those adversely affected will also find little solace in the thought that the U.S. is not the only country to be affected or in the belief that all of this has happened before.

From the perspective of individual employees, redeployment is easier said than done. As Ron Hira of the Institute of Electrical and Electronic Engineers (IEEE) asks, how realistic is it to expect a twenty-year engineering veteran to find employment as a nurse? And how many of the 32,000 workers displaced by U.S. furniture makers over the last two and one-half years—some with highly specialized skills—are likely to find employment, and where? It is true that exports create jobs, but the U.S. happens to run an enormous merchandise trade deficit. Some say this deficit does not matter but others, including this author, disagree. Furthermore, as numerous studies have shown, the jobs created by exports seldom go to those workers displaced by imports; close to one-third of the manufacturing employees displaced by foreign competition were unable to find a job. Two-thirds of those able to find work made less than in their old jobs, and while the average earnings loss was 13 percent, one-quarter suffered earning losses in excess of 30 percent. Those who found employment in the service sector, where average wages are barely more than half the manufacturing wages and where newcomers lack know-how and seniority, suffered an especially steep drop.[15]

States like Ohio, with a high concentration of manufacturing, are especially vulnerable to job loss. Policy Matters Ohio, a nonprofit and nonpartisan research institute, input data from the TAA and the former North American Free Trade Agreement (NAFTA) TAA program into an EPI economic model that takes into account exports as well as imports. The institute's study identified more than 45,000 jobs that were lost to trade competition between January 1995 and October 2003. More than three-quarters of the losses occurred in the 1999 to 2003 period, with the manufacturing wage bill in the second quarter of 2003 down $1.21 billion from three years earlier. While China's (like any other country except Canada and Mexico) generated trade displacement was not included in the study, the Federal Reserve Bank of Chicago notes that the key sectors in the Midwest economy (such as automotive) have recently become exposed to Chinese competition, with companies like Nippert (see Chapter 6, "The Business Challenge") hard hit. Job losses vary widely within the state; they were especially high in urban counties such as Cuyahoga (5,460 job losses) and almost nonexistent in Geauga and Seneca (10 job losses each). Still, only three of Ohio's congressional districts experienced less than 1,000 job losses. While those numbers should be counted against trade and investment related job gains, the comparison is not necessarily comforting: Bureau of Economic Analysis data cited by the Organization for International Investment suggests that 242,000 Ohioans are employed by foreign subsidiaries, but this number should be evaluated against outward foreign investment by Ohio companies for which domestic displacement numbers are unavailable. Global Insight sees Ohio gaining almost 4,000 jobs through outsourcing in 2003 and more than 13,000 by 2008, but this is a drop in the bucket given the overall job losses in the state.

The Economics of Job Migration

Job migration is driven primarily (but by no means only) by the prospect of lowering input cost, which helps firms remain competitive, increase margins, and tap additional revenues and opportunities that would not have been pursued otherwise.[16] Cost is not comprised only of wages (in a certain product category, labor represents less than 10 percent of product cost), nor is cost the only decision criterion when it comes to investment location; tax and regulatory environment, proximity to customers, and the availability of expertise are also important when considering investment location. In essence, companies are considering three sets of factors: the conditions at the destination (such as investment incentives, tax regime); the conditions at the departure point (such as unit costs); and the costs involved in shutting down production at the origin point (such as severance) and shifting it to destination, including the expenditure involved in coordinating design, production, distribution, and sales flows. For instance, compared to other countries, shutting down a plant is relatively easy in the U.S. The U.S. employment protection legislation is the least strict of the industrialized nations, ranking a mere 0.2 on the 1999 OECD index before New Zealand (0.4), the United Kingdom (0.5), Canada (0.6), and Ireland (0.9). Most EU countries scored high: Germany scored 2.5, France scored 3.0, and Italy scored 3.3. Spain and Portugal—two countries that are in direct competition with China for some labor intensive goods (such as shoes)—had the high scores of 3.1 and 3.7, respectively. Japan and Korea scored 2.4 and 2.6, respectively.[17] Thus, shifting production from those countries is much more expensive and cumbersome than it is in the U.S., reducing the incentive to move manufacturing away (keep in mind, however, that most EU countries have much higher unemployment rates than the U.S., partially as a result of this same inflexibility).

Exhibit 7-1 shows average hourly pay in manufacturing for selected countries in 2001 (employer cost, including bonuses and all direct pay and mandated insurance). At 30(!) times the China figure, the Chinese option looks very attractive to American producers—especially those in labor-intensive industries. In fact, moving production to China can be so attractive as to nullify the advantage of automation or of higher productivity. The gap is also sufficiently attractive vis-à-vis the labor costs in other developing markets (such as Brazil), even those that benefit from proximity to the American market (such as Mexico). But, is this gap enough to make a difference in industries where labor is not the key cost factor? For instance, according to the International Trade Commission (ITC), direct labor constitutes a mere $22 of the $469 total cost of manufacturing a TV set in the U.S., with raw materials (also much cheaper in China) constituting the main expense at $392. However, when you add a factory overhead cost of $55 (which also has a labor cost component) to direct labor, the combined dollar amount represents more than 15 percent of the final product cost (not including distribution and sales expense). Given the huge pay differential between China and the U.S., this cost impact is significant though less so when you compare China and Mexico—which, combined with transportation costs, explains why some makers of large appliances remain in Mexico while increasingly using Chinese components.

U.S.	$21.33
Europe (b)	20.18
Japan	18.83
Korea	9.16
Singapore	7.27
Taiwan	5.41
Brazil	2.57
Mexico	2.35
China	.69

a Employer cost including bonuses and mandated insurance.
b Average for Austria, Belgium, Denmark, Finland, France, Germany, Greece, Ireland, Italy, Luxembourg, Netherlands, Norway, Portugal, Spain, Sweden, Switzerland, and the UK.

Source: Bureau of Labor Statistics; China Statistical Yearbook.

Exhibit 7-1   Hourly Pay in Manufacturing 2002 (a).

The magnitude of the wage gaps suggests that currency alignment—even at the high-end estimates of 40 percent—will hardly change the equation for labor-intensive industries in the industrialized world, though it might make a difference in technology-intensive sectors and developing economies. While U.S. manufacturing productivity is five-times higher than productivity in China, the difference is not enough to compensate for a thirty-times higher wage differential. Also, the productivity gap is likely to narrow as more foreign multinationals open up shop in China and as Chinese firms invest in capital equipment and upgrade employee skills (generally speaking, productivity improvements on the low end are easier because they involve existing machinery and proven techniques).

China's labor cost advantage extends to technology-related jobs. In 2002, the average salary for a Chinese engineer was only $8,135—a 16 percent increase from 2001, but still eight-times cheaper than average U.S. levels. *The Wall Street Journal* cited internal IBM documents showing a total hourly cost (inclusive of benefits) of $12.50 for a Chinese low level programmer versus $56 for a comparable U.S. employee, or $24 versus $81 for a project manager (the figures reflect internal company accounting rather than market prices but are indicative of the company's perceived gap, which normally would take into account differences in productivity and transaction costs).[18] While wages for skilled engineers in China have been rising as a result of intense competition for talent, they are kept in check by the increasing supply of newly minted engineering graduates (almost half a million annually) and a continuous influx of technical talent from rural cities. Chinese competition may have already been exerting downward pressure on salaries across the region; average salaries for engineers across Asia were down $200 between 2001 and 2002. In the U.S., the IEEE blames foreign competition for the unprecedented seven-percent unemployment rate registered among electrical and electronic engineers in the first quarter of 2003.

Here We Go Again?

Most economists view job migration as a part of a natural progression involving redeployment of resources, assets, and capabilities and consider this progression beneficial to all economies. Over centuries, nations competed on efficiencies generated by advances in machinery and production techniques on the one hand and cheaper labor (often a function of immigration waves) on the other. "The loss of manufacturing jobs is just another chapter of technological progress in our economy," said Christopher Meyer, the former director of the Center for Business Innovation, to the conference board.[19] The U.S. (in this view) is simply ahead of the curve, experiencing structural transformation from an industrial to a service economy, akin to the transformation from agriculture to manufacturing a century earlier (see Exhibit 7-2). According to the Bureau of Labor Statistics, the number of Americans employed in the manufacturing sector today is about the same as it was more than half a century ago—except that manufacturing employment now represents barely 11 percent, versus more than one-third of nonfarm employment back then. At the same time, though its share in the economy continues to go down, the real value of manufacturing has increased.

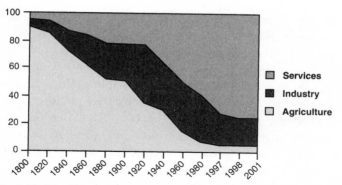

Source: *Historical Statistics of the United States: Colonial Times to 1970.* Susan Carter, Scott Gartner, Michael R. Haines, Alan Olmstead, Richard Sutch, Gavin Wright, eds. Cambridge University Press (2001).

Exhibit 7-2 Changes in U.S. Employment by Sector (1800-2001).

In an oft-cited study, Joseph Carson of Alliance Capital Management suggests that the loss of two million manufacturing jobs in the U.S. between 1995 and 2002 is part of a general trend and that other nations suffered a greater loss. China, for one, has lost 15 percent of its manufacturing employment during the same time period.[20] The numbers are accurate, but do not tell the whole story. First, as noted by the National Association of Manufacturers (NAM), China has actually added 2.5 million manufacturing jobs in the more recent 2000-2003 period. Second, as later acknowledged by Alliance Capital, the China statistics mask two divergent trends: manufacturing job losses in the inefficient and noncompetitive state sector, which has been going through a precipitous decline (from a 34 percent share of manufacturing employment in 1995 to a little over 20 percent in 1999, according to Chinese data), and job gains in the more efficient private and foreign invested enterprises that are much more competitive in world markets. The OECD notes that China, as a whole, has a much higher proportion of people employed in industry than nations at a similar level of development.

Erica Groshen and Simon Potter of the Federal Reserve Bank of New York observed that "the failure of employment to rebound during the 2001 recovery reflects an unusually high concentration of structural changes resulting in permanent shifts in the distribution of workers throughout the economy." Reasons for the structural changes include prior overexpansion, monetary and fiscal policy that has reduced cyclical change, and new management strategies focused on leaner staffing models. Trade was not included as a variable in the study, though Groshen believes that it was responsible for only a modest portion of the structural change.[21] Groshen views the U.S. as an innovating country, which explains why it sells more in developed countries than in developing markets like China and agrees that having a manufacturing base is important for retaining innovative capacity (she believes that the U.S. has lost very little of this base). While Groshen holds that we have seen significant structural change, some economists go much further. For instance, both Sung Won Sohn (chief economist of Wells Fargo) and Stephen Roach (chief economist of Morgan Stanley) see globalization as bringing about a "paradigm shift," a structural change that is unprecedented and believe that its impact is still difficult to grasp.

China and the Global Labor Market

America, then a young colony with a labor cost advantage, got textile jobs at the expense of then-costly England. Japan did the same in the later nineteenth and early twentieth century only to be followed by—in their turn—Korea, Taiwan, Singapore, and Hong Kong. On their heels came Malaysia, Indonesia, and the Philippines. The countries that lost textile jobs typically moved to bigger and better things, with some— like the U.S.—moving to the top of the table and parlaying their early economic gains into capability building in other, more advanced areas. While there were exceptions (for example, textile machinery gave England an edge over cheaper India in the nineteenth century), this was by and large the historical pattern. Is there anything new about China? The answer is unequivocally "Yes." China's enormous labor reserve, with pay scales radically lower in the hinterland than on the coast and in urban areas (the average income on the farm, where more than half of the Chinese population lives, is less than $25 per month), creates the equivalent of a country within a country; so, instead of Vietnam or Bangladesh replacing China as a labor intensive haven, Hunan will replace Guangdong. In the meantime, there are 150 million or so rural migrants in temporary employment and at least 30 million underemployed state-enterprises workers which cap wage increases.

Given its population growth (China is now relaxing its one child policy), China needs to create almost 15 million new jobs annually just to stay level and stave off an increase in the unemployment rate. Despite the demand for talent, half of 2003 college graduates in China are still looking for work. Finally, China—which comes to the global stage at a time when communication and logistic advances as well as global market liberalization facilitate the integration of production networks and supply chains globally—has no intention of playing the role of the low cost, low value-added role that the American economists have assigned to it for long. This means that it will soon be competing for the higher value-added jobs that were once considered the birthright of the industrialized world.

China's Job Impact

Calculating China's impact on the job market in the U.S. and other countries is a difficult exercise. In addition to the undercounting involved in the TAA numbers and (until recently) the lack of country specification (other than Canada and Mexico), establishing a correlation between trade and job loss or gain is tenuous because it is impossible to control all other contributing factors. Estimates regarding China's impact on U.S. manufacturing employment consequently vary. For instance, Lont Yongtu, a former vice-minister in China's Ministry of Foreign Trade and Economic Cooperation, suggested that only 10 percent of U.S. unemployment was attributable to foreign trade.[22] Jonathan Andersen, chief Asia economist at investment house UBS argues that low wage competition from Asia accounts for no more than one-twentieth of manufacturing losses in the U.S. and Japan.[23] In contrast, a Minnesota-state backed economic development group estimates that China was responsible for a significant portion of the more than 38,000 manufacturing jobs lost in the state since 2000.[24]

An interpretation of Lori Kletzer's results (published by the conservative Institute for International Economics) in light of China's exports to the U.S., suggests a potentially pronounced impact. Kletzer estimates bigger displacement impact in manufacturing—where Chinese exports are concentrated—than in services, especially when accompanied by lower import prices (a hallmark of Chinese imports). Manufacturing employees displaced from import competing industries where Chinese imports are rising fast (such as apparel, textiles, and electrical machinery) are less likely to find employment than employees displaced from other manufacturing lines. Kletzer also reports that earning losses are greater for displaced employees who fail to secure reemployment in their own industry, a more likely scenario for those competing in areas where Chinese imports are quickly cornering the market (such as clothing and electronics). Finally, the employees in the industries already involved in head-to-head competition with China (such as textiles, apparel, and leather products)—older, female, and with little education—also happen to be the most vulnerable in terms of reemployment and earning losses.

An especially somber assessment of China's job impact comes from Robert Scott of the Economic Policy Institute (EPI), a liberal think tank. Scott calculated the overall impact of China trade on U.S. employment based on the forecast of 80 percent growth in the U.S. trade deficit with China between 1999 and 2010 (a conservative assumption in light of recent trade figures), assuming full Chinese compliance with the Permanent Normal Trade Relations Agreement (an optimistic assumption). The analysis shows a net loss of almost 700,000 jobs in the 1992 to 1999 period and a projected loss of almost 900,000 jobs in the 1999 to 2010 period; total job losses fall at close to 740,000 and 1,150,000, respectively (see Exhibit 7-3).

U.S. Trade with China, 1992-1999			Change from 1992-1999		
	1992	1999	Dollars	Percent	Jobs Lost or Gained
Exports	$ 6,702	$ 11,329	$ 4,627	69%	56,129
Imports	23,219	70,075	46,856	202%	−739,361
Trade Balance	-16,516	−58,746	−42,228	256%	**−683,231**

U.S. Trade with China, 1999-2010			Change from 1999-2010		
	1999	2010	Dollars	Percent	Jobs Lost or Gained
Exports	$ 11,329	$ 32,648	$ 21,319	188%	276,221
Imports	70,075	138,651	68,575	98%	−1,148,313
Trade Balance	−58,746	−106,002	−47,256	80%	**−872,091**

Source: Scott, Robert. China and the States. Briefing Paper, the Economic Policy Institute (2003).

Exhibit 7-3 Total Job Losses from Growing U.S. Trade Deficits with China, 1992-2010 (Millions of Constant 1987 Dollars in Units of 1,000).

Not surprisingly, Scott projects that manufacturing will bear the brunt of China-generated job losses with over 740,000 net job losses, 85 percent of the estimated total. No sector is forecasted to gain jobs, though selected players will. For instance, though agriculture as a whole will lose jobs, Scott notes that agribusiness concerns will benefit because they earn from both exports and imports of agricultural products. The labor-intensive sector, already in decline, will see a dramatic acceleration in job losses. Labor Department figures show that textile mill employment in the U.S. declined from 477,700 in January 1993 to 284,000 in December 2002. *Business Week* reported a loss of nearly 50,000 U.S.-based garment and textile jobs in 2003, but the carnage is expected to get much worse. The Union of Needletrades, Industrial, and Textile Employees (UNITE) forecasts a loss of half a million textile and apparel jobs once the multifiber agreement expires in 2004; the Textile Manufacturers Institute puts the number at 630,000 between 2004 and 2006 alone. The Institute projects that, assuming a 65 percent market penetration of Chinese products, roughly two-thirds of U.S. workers employed in the textile trade and its supporting industries may lose their jobs.

	Jobs Gained from Growth of Total Exports	Jobs Lost from Growth of Total Imports	Net Jobs Lost Due to Change in Trade Balance
Agriculture Forestry, Fisheries	23,631	-28,726	-5,095
Mining	3,917	-6,675	-2,758
Construction	2,692	-7,564	-4,872
Manufacturing	189,841	-932,041	-742,201
Transportation	11,486	31,709	-20,223
Communications	1,800	-5,748	-3,948
Utilities	2,737	-7,208	-4,471
Trade	3,952	-14,768	-10,816
Finance, Insurance, Real Estate	6,754	-19,604	-12,850
Services	26,725	-85,116	-58,391
Government	2,687	-9,153	-6,467
TOTAL	276,221	-1,148,313	-872,091
Manufacturing Share Total	68.7%	81.2%	85.1%

Source: Scott, Robert. China and the States. Economic Policy Institute (2003).

Exhibit 7-4 Job Losses by Industry under the China-World Trade Organization Proposal 1999-2010.

Because of their industry correlates, job losses will also vary by state. As shown in Exhibit 7-5, future losses will be dramatically higher in states that rely on manufacturing (such as Ohio), versus those that are more dependent on agriculture (such as Iowa) or that are in other sectors of the economy (such as Louisiana). Hawaii, which relies heavily on tourism and federal spending, may actually benefit from China's rise if an influx of Chinese tourists materializes and if it picks up military expenditure should China stir up trouble in the Taiwan Strait.

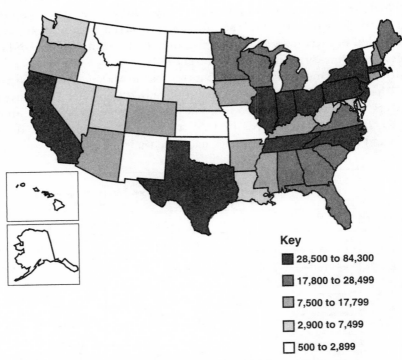

Key

■ 28,500 to 84,300

▨ 17,800 to 28,499

▧ 7,500 to 17,799

▢ 2,900 to 7,499

□ 500 to 2,899

Source: Scott, Robert. China and the States. Working Paper, Economic Policy Institute (2003).

Exhibit 7-5   Job Losses by State under the China-WTO Proposal (1999-2010).

States with a significant number of apparel-related jobs will be hit especially hard. The Textile Manufacturers Institute estimated job losses ranging from 85,000 in North Carolina to 25,000 in Georgia, for a total of 630,000 U.S. jobs. Particularly grim are the prospects of apparel employees in states like North and South Carolina, where overall manufacturing unemployment already exceeds 15 percent. Those workers face dim reemployment prospects not only in their own industry but also in the manufacturing sector as a whole and, hence, face grim prospects for employment and—should they find a job—for earning retention.

As bad as the impact will be in the developed world, it will be much worse in developing nations, especially those that rely on the apparel industry for much of their foreign earnings. As noted in *Business Week*, a Chinese clothing worker makes, on average, $73 per month versus $300 in Honduras. Wages in Indonesia ($75 a month) and the Dominican Republican ($102, but discounted by a distance advantage) are more comparable, yet those countries are still projected to suffer enormous job losses; for instance, the Dominican Republic is forecasted to lose one-third of its 119,000 garment workers.[25] This is because the Chinese now employ advanced production techniques and can extract the benefits of agglomeration with end product and supporting industries networked in the same locale. While the impact will be mitigated by recent U.S. trade initiatives, it is doubtful that Central American and Caribbean nations will remain competitive in the apparel sector for long.

Is Your Job in Jeopardy?

As a kid, your parents may have prodded you to finish your meal because there was a hungry child in China or India who would love to have it. In the coming years, you may hear from your boss that a Chinese or Indian employee is hungry for your job. So, how vulnerable are you? Let's start with a broad brush: If you are in manufacturing, there is a better than 50/50 chance that your job is at risk. The manufacturing sector has been shedding jobs for years, and now offers fewer jobs than it did more a generation ago despite a sizable increase in the population base. The trends that kept a lid on employment in this sector— productivity, technological improvements, and foreign competition—are all accelerating. As a result, U.S. manufacturing has lost 13 percent of its workforce over the last three years alone. In labor-intensive and noncomplex assembly jobs, the writing is already on the wall. The Federal Reserve Bank of New York's Erica Groshen and Simon Potter found a significant job decline in industries where China is a major exporter to the U.S.: apparel (–9.14% in the most recent recession), electronics and electrical equipment (–12.04%), leather and leather products (–12.5%), and furniture (–8.16%). All indications are that job losses in those segments will pick up speed in the years ahead. For example, if you are a textile mill worker in North Carolina, your prospects for retaining employment beyond 2008 (when special World Trade Organization (WTO) provisions allowing remedy against import surge expire) are not at all promising.

The impact of China implies not only a deepening but also a broadening of job losses. Kletzer reports that the share of white collar employees among those displaced in the U.S. manufacturing sector has been on the increase, from 29.9 percent in the 1979 to 1989 period to 35.3 percent in the 1990 to 1999 period. The proportion is likely to increase as China, India, and other developing nations offer skilled staff at a fraction of domestic cost and as technological developments and logistic advances facilitate off-shoring. Off-shoring proponents like to point out that the phenomenon currently accounts for a minute portion of job displacement but they rarely note that it joins other forms of job migration, such as trade displacement, which together account for a significant portion of overall job losses in the economy. These proponents of off-shoring also fail to note that these channels (off-shoring, trade displacement, and so on), too, see growing white-collar losses. It is the flight of skilled, white-collar jobs—especially those that are knowledge intensive, such as research and development—that is shaking the belief in the overall benefit of job migration.

Politics and Policies

At this junction, it is outsourcing rather than the much more significant trade displacement that is the focus of the political debate surrounding the loss of jobs to foreign competition. Just how charged this issue has become was illustrated when President Bush's chief economic advisor belatedly expressed understanding with those losing jobs to outsourcing and when the president's nominee for manufacturing czar was forced to withdraw when it was found that his own company has outsourced to China. The vast majority of interviewees in a DiamondCluster survey were concerned with political backlash regarding outsourcing, but employers are apparently not concerned with the reaction of their workers: 80 percent of the respondents in a Gartner survey said that their off-shoring plans will not be affected by potential opposition from workers.

Policy initiatives devised to tackle job migration range from the punitive (such as limiting U.S. government agencies' help to off-shoring firms or levying a higher tax rate on off-shoring companies) to the supportive (such as providing funds for retraining, broadening the definition of jobs under TAA) and the administrative (such as reducing the number of visas issued to foreign workers with special skills). Most of those initiatives are likely to face stiff opposition on the part of business groups that have become dependent on foreign production and outsourcing. Another set of ideas is designed to protect those adversely affected: This includes proposals by Kletzer and Robert Litan (of the Brookings Institute) to require earning loss insurance and by Glenn Hubbard (the former chairman of the Council of Economic Advisors under Bush), to establish "reemployment accounts."[26] Policy initiative notwithstanding, employees will do best by understanding the nature of the coming changes and their impact.

Navigating the New Job Landscape

Should you steer clear of the labor-intensive sectors of the economy? Not necessarily. According to Bardhan and Kroll, the jobs that are likely to withstand outsourcing are those that require either face-to-face contact with a customer or social networking requirements, do not involve pay that would be much lower in an alternate location, have high setup barriers, and/or cannot be easily communicated via technology. Some of those jobs have already proven their resilience, such as personal services (0.00% in the Groshen and Potter data) and legal services (+2.24%). Jobs such as being a waiter or firefighter require workers to be present and are, therefore, relatively safe. In contrast, some personal-service jobs seem safe from outsourcing but can be staffed by imported workers. Even construction, one of the last strongholds of unionized America, is on the line: new construction techniques (such as modular assembly) mean that a portion of the job can be done overseas. While the healthcare sector is growing (+2.09% in the Groshen and Potter data), the market for nurses is rapidly becoming global. Medical services such as record transcription are being outsourced and patient mobility is growing despite regulatory and insurance hurdles. The same is true for airline pilots: Preparing for a strike standoff, Hong Kong-based Cathay

Pacific has lined up mainland Chinese crews and planes to fill in at a much lower cost structure. While certification and union agreements prevent that from occurring in most other countries, such a scenario is not farfetched once the aviation market liberalizes further.

In contrast, supply chain jobs such as those in shipping, logistic services, and distribution will benefit from increased movement of goods and services across borders. Education jobs, such as trainers and professors, will be needed to train Chinese employees (including the most dreaded job of training Chinese or Indian workers to take your place) and to keep the innovation edge. Tourism is also likely to greatly benefit from an influx of Chinese tourists. Finally, there will be opportunities in the Chinese labor market: Shanghai's Liberation Daily recently reported that 1,200 Japanese managers and engineers applied for work in the city.[27]

Up (or Down) the Ladder

In its 2004-2005 Occupational Outlook, forecasting job growth between 2002 and 2012, the U.S. Department of Labor lists thirty occupations as offering the brightest prospects. Of those, five are in healthcare (such as nurses, home health aides) and four are in education (such as teacher assistants). Next, however, are three food service categories (such as waiters). Jobs as security guards, janitors and repairmen, and sales clerks and truck drivers subsequently follow—not exactly the twenty-first century jobs that you may have had in mind. Only three of the jobs are managerial (including managerial analysts) and only two are technologically intensive (including computer service engineers).

Indeed, perhaps the most dramatic employment challenge of the Chinese century is that education is no longer the insurance policy against trade displacement and other forms of job migration it once was. As the IEEE's Ron Hira noted in his testimony before the House Small Business Committee, in the thirty years in which the Department of Labor has collected such statistics, the unemployment rate for electrical and electronic engineers has never exceeded that of the general unemployment rate. That is, until now. Much of the U.S. technological edge rests on an influx of talent from abroad that in the future may seek other venues and, despite great efforts, the U.S. educational system is not exactly a model of readiness for the new technology frontiers: According to the National Center for Educational Statistics, the math test scores of 13-year-olds in the U.S. rank 31 out of 35 participating nations and provinces—ahead only of the French population of Ontario, Jordan, two Brazilian provinces, and Mozambique. China ranks first, Taiwan third. Truly, the U.S. has some great universities, but it would be a dangerous mistake to take the current innovation lead for granted. The arrogant comment of MIT's career services director that "the jobs that are being outsourced aren't the jobs that (its) students are seeking"[28] may come back to haunt us all.

Take, for example, electronic chips. Interviewed in Fortune magazine, Lin Stiles of the executive search firm Linford Stiles and Associates, declared that for high tech firms, "...product design and marketing really have to stay in the U.S. [and]...aren't getting outsourced."[29] She should not be so sure. Israeli scientists already do groundbreaking chip development for Intel and may do so for others in the future. China, in the meantime, is offering significant tax rebates for companies to locate chip design on its soil. Hewlett-Packard already designs computer servers in Singapore and in Taiwan, and there is no reason to believe it will not eventually do so on the mainland. And, as far as marketing is concerned, why is it preordained to stay in the U.S. when many markets abroad (such as China) are growing faster? In an age of global supply chains, the organizational "brain" will be staffed with people who understand other cultures and environments. American diversity helps greatly in this respect, but business education that is increasingly devoid of any country specific information does not.

The increasing complexity of the global labor environment suggests that we do not take old assumptions for granted. In the words of Wachovia Securities chief economist John Silvia, "...because of the globalization of the labor market, the relationship between economic growth and employment is different this time than it has been in the past...in other words, the models are permanently broken."[30] China will play a central role in how the new models turn out, and we'd better be prepared.

8

A TV from Sichuan

To the consumer, China's entry into global markets seems at first sight to be tracking the road traveled by Japan and later by South Korea, Taiwan, and Hong Kong. Both Japan and the tigers (South Korea, Taiwan, Hong Kong, and Singapore) initially flooded global markets with low-quality, cheap products, priced well below those of domestic producers and other foreign competitors. With quality and reliability improving, prices were kept in check or rose modestly, forming a value proposition that global customers could not ignore. The range of exports then gradually expanded to cover broader product categories, mostly by way of moving up market (for example, from a simple transistor radio to a stereo radio-tape). The more generous margins in the upper segments allowed better return while preserving price advantage over established competitors. In the process, the low end was relinquished to lower-cost newcomers.

China's path shows many of the same features, but also some remarkable differences. While Japan and Korea gradually exited the cheap-good segments in favor of capturing the higher margins available

145

from higher-end products, China has begun moving into the high end without deserting the low-end. Chinese furniture, for example, now covers the entire range—from the "low" to the "better" to the "best" segments of the U.S. household furniture market. The same is true for color television sets, where Chinese makers continue to dominate the conventional receiver segment while extending their product range upward and often leapfrogging into advanced (and higher-margin) plasma sets. The breadth of offering is especially attractive to the large-scale U.S. importers and retailers who are looking for a one-stop shop for diverse and changing procurement needs.

In addition to offering a broader scope of products at an early stage, China has been quicker than its predecessors to penetrate global markets. It did so first by leveraging a much larger foreign-investment tide and relying on the exports of multinationals with advanced technology, established brand names, existing distribution channels, and intimate knowledge of global markets. By observing and supplying the multinational players, Chinese producers developed strong Original Equipment Manufacturer (OEM) capabilities and circumvented the costly need to build brand identity, distribution, and service networks instead selling under somebody else's label—whether that of an established manufacturer, a retailer's private label, or the producer's own untested brand. The Chinese onslaught occurs at a time when the U.S. retail sector has come to be dominated by giant retail discounters, with China both a beneficiary and a cause of this transformation. According to the International Trade Commission (ITC), the top five retailers now account for 65–70 percent of the U.S. market for conventional color televisions receivers—up from about 40 percent ten years ago. Discounters (such as Wal-Mart, Target, Best Buy, and Circuit City) compete on price and are willing to make their shelves available to relatively unknown brands. They primarily seek low cost but also require reliability, short lead time, and vast production capacity—a combination that inevitably leads to China. Similar trends can be observed in Japan, where discounters such as the 100-yen stores have been among the most enthusiastic importers of Chinese merchandise (Europe—whose retail market remains fairly fragmented—is somewhat behind, though this is changing as well). However, while the Japanese have a favorable attitude toward their domestic products regardless of product superiority, Americans evaluate a domestic product more favorably only when it has superior qualities.[1] Thus, the American market and the China production machine seem like a match made in heaven.

Related to the rise of large retailers, and critical to the penetration of Chinese products into global markets, is the decline of the brand. With staple consumer products such as TV sets and DVD players turning into commodities, the appeal of any but the strongest and most exclusive brands has considerably eroded. America's Research Group found that, between 2000 and 2003, the percentage of shoppers who said that brands were extremely important in their purchase decision declined from 48 to 32 percent.[2] Chinese manufacturers have been prime beneficiaries of this changing sentiment. That the rise of giant retailers and the decline in brand consciousness have been more pronounced in the U.S. than in Europe partially explains why the U.S. has thus far borne the brunt of Chinese imports.

The U.S. consumer has shown an insatiable appetite for Chinese products—from bicycles, coats, and Christmas ornaments to TV sets and DVD players. In 1992, China had less than 10 percent of the U.S. electronics market. By the end of the decade, that had more than doubled. TCL is set to become the world's largest TV maker with Changhong, Konka, and others following. As China expands and upgrades its product lines, its relentless march into foreign markets picks up pace. Potential resistance, if it comes, will probably be rooted in the political and social ramifications of China's rise rather than in the change in economic fundamentals. Despite sporadic efforts by U.S. unions and a number of grass root groups (such as Mad in the USA), a clear link between the consumer and the employee role is yet to be established. If such a link were to be established, a backlash not unlike that associated with the Japanese exports of the 1980s could follow with far reaching consequences for all players.

The Factory to the World Meets the Consumer of the World

The preponderance of Chinese products, from clothing and furniture to electronics and appliances, on the world's retail shelves illustrates how fast Chinese imports are capturing market share from domestic products as well as from third-country producers. The trend has been especially pronounced in the U.S., where China's share of U.S. imports has been growing steadily (see Exhibit 8-1). There is no indication that this export drive is going to stop any time soon; on the contrary, all indications are that it will continue to grow at a brisk pace and—in some instances—reach what trade regulations refer to as "surges."

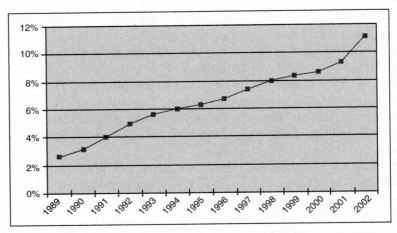

Source: *Direction of Trade Statistics, International Financial Statistics*, International Monetary Fund, 2003.

Exhibit 8-1   U.S. Imports from China as a Percent of Total Imports.

Chinese makers of wooden bedroom furniture were in an ideal position to take advantage of the U.S. retail opportunities. According to the ITC, 97.3 percent of Chinese household furniture imports in the U.S. went directly to retailers (versus 90 percent for domestic makers), mostly under private store labels—something U.S. producers, apparently, were not ready to do. Importers noted that reliability, consistent quality, short lead time, timely delivery, production capacity, product range, and customization capabilities provided an edge to Chinese products beyond a mere price advantage. It is especially interesting that customization, once a barrier to importers, has become a competitive advantage of Chinese products. Both state-of-the-art machinery and skilled craftsmanship are noted in different parts of the ITC report as providing Chinese makers with a competitive advantage, but it is the combination of the two that confers the real advantage over competitors who typically have one but not the other. Domestic-producer advantages in lower shipping costs and order lead time were not as obvious. For instance, the ITC figures show an average order lead time of 29.5 days for domestic manufacturers versus 80 days for Chinese imports, but importers supplying from U.S. inventory had an average lead time of only 15 days.

In the TV market, Chinese manufacturers have moved quickly from an also-ran to a dominant player, capturing market share not only from domestic producers (ironically, only one of the seven "domestic" U.S. producers listed in the ITC investigation, Tennessee-based Five Rivers, is not foreign owned, and Five Rivers itself assembles sets for Korean maker Samsung and Dutch maker Phillips), but also from third-country competitors. For instance, Commerce Department figures show that while the value of Malaysian-made TV sets sold in the U.S. has almost doubled between 1998 and 2002 (from $1.04 billion to $1.97 billion), Chinese imports rose six-fold (from $685.27 million to $ 4.28 billion) during the same period.

The TV industry was an ideal point of entry for Chinese manufacturers. The basic technology was widely available, and several developed-country television-makers (such as GE and Motorola) had exited the low-margin business years earlier. Chinese companies, such as Sichuan-based Changhong Electric, have cut their teeth battling with the likes of Matsushita and Toshiba in their domestic market and then turned their attention to global markets. In addition to a lower cost structure, rapid growth in their domestic market helped Chinese producers obtain scale advantages, and hence lower unit costs, that other producers found impossible to match. At the request of domestic U.S. manufacturers, the ITC has recently looked at import of color TV sets from both China and Malaysia. In June 2003, the ITC determined that there was a reasonable indication of material injury to the U.S. industry from the import of certain color TV receivers.

The Nation of Wal-Mart

A key reason behind the remarkably fast penetration of Chinese products into the U.S. market is a retail landscape increasingly dominated by large retailers. These retailers are more price sensitive, require massive production capacity and short lead time to accommodate changing tastes or massive promotions, and possess the global supply chains that facilitate import logistics. They also have the market presence and scale necessary to sell an untested brand either under their own private label or under that of a neophyte manufacturer. Take Wal-Mart, the world's largest retailer (and largest company), which accounts for more than 10 percent of U.S. imports from China. It has been estimated that Wal-Mart bought upwards of $12 billion worth of Chinese goods in 2002, making it not only the largest buyer of Chinese goods in America but a bigger importer of made-in-China products than Canada, the UK, or France (see Exhibit 8-2). Unofficial figures for 2003 put Wal-Mart's China purchases at $15 billion.

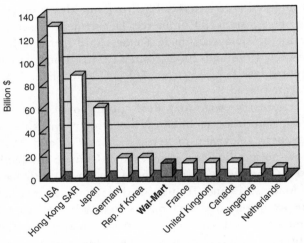

Source: UN COMTRADE, *Business Week* (October 6, 2003).

Exhibit 8-2   Imports from China (2002).

Wal-Mart's purchases from China received much attention not only because of the size of the retailer and the magnitude of its imports, but also because they came on the hills of its 1980s "Bring It Home to the USA" campaign which was derailed when the media challenged the country of origin of some its merchandise, as well as the conditions under which it was produced. The retailer subsequently adopted the position that it "buys American whenever it can," but it would be years before the company would specify what this meant—that if a U.S.-made product would fall within 5 percent of the price and quality of an imported competitor, Wal-Mart would take smaller markup and go with the American product. By the 1990s, however, foreign imports and (in particular) Chinese products came in at a much larger margin and Wal-Mart was on its way toward becoming China's number one import retailer. The company has a major purchasing operation in Shenzhen (a post-reform city adjacent to Hong Kong) whose representatives are scurrying the country for buying opportunities.

China fits very well with Wal-Mart strategy of "everyday low prices" coupled with huge promotions, which bring masses of shoppers into its stores for one-time events. According to the ITC, everyday sales account for most of Wal-Mart's TV sales but only a small percentage of its imports. Wal-Mart typically orders huge numbers of imported TVs for special promotions and told the ITC that, immaterial of price, no domestic producer could have met the huge scale of products it needed for such sale events. For its Thanksgiving 2002 "blitz," Wal-Mart contracted with Sichuan-based Changhong Electric to supply thousands of TV sets sold under the Apex Digital brand.

The increasing share of large retailers like Wal-Mart, and the increasingly prominent role China plays in their plans, suggests continuous pressure on manufacturers throughout the world and a growing presence of Chinese goods on retail shelves. With Chinese dominance of apparel, toys, and consumer electronics markets, fewer and fewer non-Chinese firms will be able to provide the scale, product scope, lead time, and price that the large retailers seek. The Chinese, on their side, need the large retailers to take their growing production capacity—at least until they are able to develop their own distribution and establish their brands. Thus, the fates of Wal-Mart and the Chinese industry will remain closely intertwined for years to come.

A Level Playing Field

One of the major arguments of importers and proponents of Chinese products is that they do not compete head-on with American-made products since they are typically found in the lower end of the product scale. A recent investigation by the ITC is informative: As part of a comprehensive assessment of Chinese competition in the household wooden furniture industry, the ITC examined what Chinese products were in competition with domestic and other foreign imports. The results presented in Exhibit 8-3 suggest competition across the board, with a majority of both domestic producers and importers of the opinion that Chinese products are always or frequently interchangeable with domestic as well as third-country products. Furthermore, the ITC believes that this is true for the furniture market as a whole.[3]

Country Pair	Number of U.S. Producers Reporting					Number of U.S. Importers Reporting				
	A	F	S	N	O	A	F	S	N	O
U.S. vs. China	29	6	2	2	---	37	11	8	4	7
U.S. vs. third countries	22	6		1	3	30	12	7	3	7
China vs. third countries	19	7	3	2	4	33	12	4	3	6

Note: A=Always, F=Frequently, S=Sometimes, N=Never, O=No Familiarity

Source: USITC #3667, January 2004.

Exhibit 8-3   Interchangeability of Chinese Wooden Bedroom Furniture in the U.S. Market.

Pricing

While Chinese products have made significant quality strides, they continue to rely on cost as a key competitive advantage. In the ITC investigation of the color TV market, Wal-Mart and Sears suggested that it was natural for the Chinese and Malaysian imports to be priced lower since they are not sold under established brands that signal quality. This was disputed by the domestic producers who argued that the product has become a commodity and that brands have become almost meaningless, with Sony the only manufacturer able to command a price premium. The domestic makers also noted that the Chinese and Malaysian imports now penetrated all segments of the TV market and did not remain confined to cheaper, entry-level models. The ITC agreed with that view, noting that many of the imports had features associated with higher-end models.

According to the ITC figures, Chinese and Malaysian sets undersold their domestic competitors in all thirty-eight possible price comparisons, with margins ranging from 1.6 to 50.3 percent. While price erosion has been a fixture of the industry over the last decade, the ITC calculated that where Chinese and Malaysian sets competed directly with domestic TVs, the erosion has been faster than the 4.3 percent average decline in the consumer price index for televisions between 1995 and 2001; the Commission thus concluded that these imports have had "a significant price depressing effect." The ITC investigation of wooden bedroom furniture shows a similar trend, with Chinese imports priced less than similar domestic products in 107 out of 108 price comparisons. The margin of difference ranged from 4.9 to 77.2 percent. Exhibit 8-4 shows, however, that while price remains the key factor supporting Chinese imports, it is by no means the only one.

Country Pair	Number of U.S. Importers Reporting					Number of U.S. Producers Reporting				
	A	F	S	N	O	A	F	S	N	O
U.S. vs. China	21	12	13	12	5	9	2	13	16	---
U.S. vs. third countries	20	9	15	6	7	6	3	13	11	3
China vs. third countries	17	9	16	8	4	3	1	5	11	12

Note: A=Always, F=Frequently, S=Sometimes, N=Never, O=No Familiarity

Source: USITC #3667, January 2004.

Exhibit 8-4 Perceived Importance of Differences Other than Price in U.S. Products vs. Chinese Imports and Third-Country Imports of Wooden Bedroom Furniture.

Would You Buy a Chinese Product?

Chinese products would not be on so many retail shelves if potential customers were not willing to buy them. Leo J. Shapiro and Associates, a Chicago-based survey research firm, studied the attitudes of Americans towards China and Chinese products in May of 2002. A nationally projected sample of 450 U.S. households were surveyed about their interest in buying Chinese products. As Exhibit 8-5 shows, the interest is moderate, with more than half of respondents showing a high- to mid-level interest but more than 40 percent not showing an interest. These proportions will probably change as Chinese products become more known and uncertainty regarding quality diminishes, though other factors (such as animosity) may dampen a growing enthusiasm.

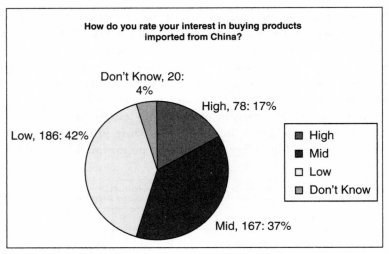

Source: Leo J. Shapiro & Associates.

Exhibit 8-5   Potential Buyer Interest in Chinese Products.

That interest is high in electronics and computers and not only in arts and clothing (see Exhibit 8-6) suggests that China is beginning to acquire a reputation for providing reasonable quality in technology products. Indeed, when people are asked why they are interested in Chinese products, cheap price still comes first but is immediately followed by positive perceptions regarding product quality and technological experience as well as by positive experience with Chinese products (see Exhibit 8-7). This perception of Chinese products as providing good quality at a reasonable price is noteworthy because it is not far from the value proposition that many global customers attach to U.S.-made products. This suggests that, down the road, made-in-China goods will be in direct competition with American products in world markets.

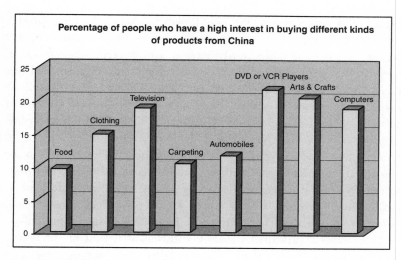

Source: Leo J. Shapiro & Associates.

Exhibit 8-6   Interest in Different Chinese Products.

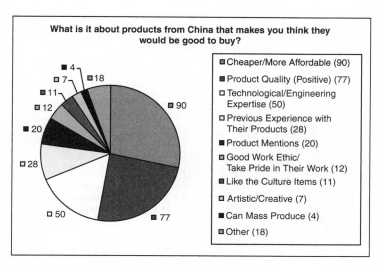

Source: Leo J. Shapiro & Associates.

Exhibit 8-7   Reasons for Buying Chinese Products.

Exhibit 8-8 lists reasons why people would *not* buy Chinese products. The exhibit suggests that poor quality remains a major concern, which is consistent with the Chinese Ministry of Commerce's observation that foreign quality standards in developed-country markets pose the biggest obstacle to increased Chinese exports. This is immediately followed, however, by nonproduct-related issues such as the perceived treatment of Chinese employees or concern for U.S. jobs—both of which also play an important role in the purchasing decision. This suggests that the decision to buy made-in-China products may become entangled in social and political considerations. Marketers know that animosity can play an important role in purchasing decisions.[4] It is quite possible that such animosity may develop toward China based on perceptions regarding anything from working conditions to geopolitical developments (say, aggression toward Taiwan). A Zogby International poll of likely voters released on September 30, 2003, shows China at the top of a list of non-allied countries, ahead of Saudi Arabia and France. An earlier poll (released June 13, 2003) found that more than 80 percent saw China as a serious threat to U.S. national security.

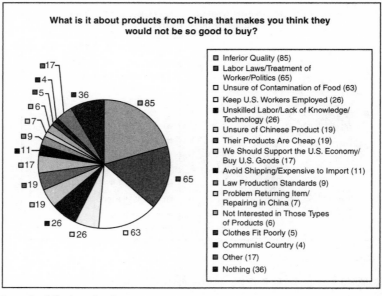

Source: Leo J. Shapiro & Associates.

Exhibit 8-8   Reasons for Not Buying Chinese Products.

Further information on the image of Chinese products comes from a study by Gary Insch in *Management International Review*.[5] Insch quizzed purchasing managers and agents in the U.S. and Mexico regarding their perceptions on the quality and design of manufacturing in various countries. The findings (see Exhibit 8-9) show that in the Mexican sample, China ranks lowest of all countries surveyed on both design and manufacturing quality. In the U.S., however, China places ahead of Mexico and Brazil and is not far from the score for Malaysia, a country that has attracted considerable manufacturing foreign investment before China.

Country	U.S. Sample (N=294)		Mexican Sample (N=183)	
	Manuf. Quality Mean Score	Design Quality Mean Score	Manuf. Quality Mean Score	Design Quality Mean Score
Japan	13.46	13.28	14.19	13.90
Germany	13.14	12.85	14.08	13.67
U.S.	12.87	13.17	13.27	13.57
Malaysia	8.74	8.14	8.77	8.27
China	**8.40**	**8.03**	**8.22**	**7.86**
Mexico	8.19	7.74	9.72	9.21
Brazil	8.06	7.78	9.18	8.85

Source: Gary S. Insch. The impact of country-of-origin effects on industrial buyers' perceptions of product quality. *Management International Review*, 43. 3, 2003, 291-310.

Exhibit 8-9 Comparative Ratings for Perceived Manufacturing and Design Quality.

China and the Brand

China has been a major beneficiary of (as well as a reason for) the decline of the brand in the retail market. According to the *Financial Times*, with the exception of super-luxury brands whose identity is intrinsically linked to European manufacturing, all others are either manufacturing in Asia or are thinking about it.[6] Asia, increasingly, means China. The Chinese themselves are nonetheless very brand conscious, a legacy of Confucian hierarchy and of their imperial past where rank was prominently displayed on bureaucrats' clothing. Chinese producers seek to escape the low-end segment of the market on its razor thin margins, ever-increasing price pressures by global buyers, and intense competition on the part of both foreign and domestic producers—including new entrants that appear in the market almost daily. One of the main escape routes involves brand building as a way to capture the higher margins of premium products. The Chinese government has also sought to support this trend with an endorsement by the Chairman of the National People's Congress and the establishment of a Chinese Brand Promotion section under the State Bureau of Quality and Technology. Building brands fits with the government's strategy of consolidating strategic industries in order to create national champions that can hold their own in global markets and is viewed as one more way for the country to restore its imperial glory.

Chinese companies such as Haier and Lenovo (formerly Legend) are already building brand names at home and abroad. Others have found a quicker and cheaper way, buying the trademarks of companies in distress (for example, TCL's acquisition of German electronic-appliance maker Schneider), taking over customers with whom they have done business as an OEM (for example, Techtronic's purchase of Cleveland-based Royal, manufacturer of the Dirt Devil and Royal brands), or via an alliance with a branded manufacturer (for example, TCL's majority ownership of a joint venture embedding Thomson's TV business with its RCA mark).

Is "Buy American" Returning?

In his book, *Buy American*,[7] Dana Frank recalls the Buy American campaign of the 1970s and 1980s, from the hacking of a Toyota in Detroit to the racial overtones of the union campaign featuring an American flag made in Japan and the "Made by an American, worn by an American, paid for by an American" hat made in China. Frank notes that union-label and crafted-with-pride campaigns floundered not only because of increased blurring of product origin (such as an Ohio-made Honda) but mostly because "the whole logic of saving jobs by buying American was dependent upon the concept of a partnership between U.S. workers and corporate allies. But the corporate part of the team—like the auto and apparel industries—was itself fleeing overseas." These lines could have been written today. With U.S. foreign investment higher than at any Japan-bashing time, major retailers relying on Chinese imports to maintain a price advantage, and major manufacturers dependent on Chinese outsourcing to stay in business, a coalition of multinationals and consumers to oppose made-in-China imports is even

less likely. Says Tom Hopson, the CEO of domestic TV maker Five
Rivers, who filed the complaint to the ITC: "I was surprised to see U.S.
retailers at the hearings. They were acting like we were filing a suit
against them."[8] Similarly, furniture retailers, increasingly dependent on
Chinese imports, threatened to exclude U.S. manufacturers who
complained about Chinese imports from their showrooms. That those
constituencies will so diverge is part of the China impact that is here
to stay.

9

China Rising

The rise of China at the dawn of the twenty-first century is not only about a flood of cheap imports, the decline of certain segments of the manufacturing sector in other countries, or the offshore transfer of jobs—as important as these trends are. It would be no exaggeration to say that China's rise is a watershed event that will change the global landscape and that is on par with the ascent of the United States of America as a global economic, political, and military power a century earlier. If current trends continue, China will surpass the U.S. to become the world's largest economy (in purchasing-power parity terms) in two decades—possibly sooner. Crossing this benchmark has little practical significance but will symbolize China's coming of age, from an economic backwater to an industrial powerhouse, and underpin its emergence as a world power. Even before this benchmark is crossed, China will become the dominant manufacturer and exporter in industries ranging from the labor intensive to the technology driven. It will also be a strong contender, though not yet a leader, in product lines associated with advanced technology and will start to play an important role in the higher end of the market. Chinese-made cars will become a common sight on American and European roads, sporting not only the familiar name brands of Ford and VW (which already sells Chinese-made cars in Australia) but also the marks of SAIC and Dongfeng Motors. Made-in-China regional jets will enter commercial aviation, and Chinese missions to space—while not leading edge—will cease to be a news item.

At stake are economic clout, global stature, and military prowess. Within a decade, China will become the hub for an east- and southeast-Asian market that will rival the economies of Europe and the Americas. It will be a broker and arbiter of global diplomatic affairs not only in Asia but the world over. Rising military prominence will allow China to counterbalance what it views as a Western-dominated world, redrawing the political and security map and turning what it sees as single player hegemony into a two- or three-player game. China will remain true to its nonexpansionist tradition, but will utilize its economic muscle in the service of a broader international and political agenda and vice versa.

The advance will not be linear. While no fan of Chairman Mao Zedong, I buy into his spring metaphor for progress—circuitous yet unequivocally pointed forward. In the coming years, China will need to transform its banking sector, diffuse a social security crisis, and respond to growing discontent on the part of laid-off and rural workers as well as other have-nots. Its leadership will walk a fine line between relaxing an autocratic political system and needing to retain effective control so as to maintain law and order and one-party rule. Fears of unemployment and resulting unrest will continue to feed its export engine, but the same fears may work to avert a trade war. To manage this acrobatic feat, China will put a premium on building and sustaining global and domestic coalitions with vested interest in open trade—for instance, enlisting foreign manufacturers who are dependent on the Chinese market for exports, production inputs, and assembly, as well as the large retailers for whom it has become a key business model ingredient.

The China impact is already visible in the form of pricing, from deflationary pressures at the retail level to inflationary pressures on raw materials and logistics. In retail, Chinese imports are squeezing the margins of all but the largest players and forcing smaller fries that lack a sophisticated supply chain out of the water. This is now apparent in product lines where China dominates (such as toys), where the likes of Wal-Mart are squeezing both small and large dedicated players. At the same time, Chinese demand is exerting upward pressures on the prices of copper, titanium, nickel, rubber, iron ore, steel, coal, and oil, and even cardboard, among other materials. The price of scrap steel—a key raw material for many U.S. producers that is now imported *en masse* by Chinese buyers—is skyrocketing, up by more than one-third just in the first quarter of 2004.

Immediate impacts aside, the aftershocks from the China impact will reverberate for years even if they are under the radar for now since they take time to evolve, are less visible, or are more difficult to discern because they involve multiple variables of which the China impact is only one. One example is the impact on pollution and global warming; another is the integration of the Asian economy with China at its hub. Still another example is a fundamental shift in global immigration flows. The China impact is therefore not a one-two punch, but rather a gradual restructuring of economy, business, and politics that will play for years and decades to come.

Misplaced Analogies

Playing down the economic impact of China's ascent on the U.S. and other developed economies, economists have repeatedly posited the analogy that America's transition from an industrial to a service economy is—in essence—a repeat of its shift a century earlier from an agricultural to an industrial economy. The analogy—used, for instance, by former labor secretary Robert Reich in a *Wall Street Journal* essay[1]—implies that the exit from multiple segments of the manufacturing sector represents a natural evolution of an economy that is ahead on the evolution curve and implies that the new companies and new jobs created as a result of the transition will be more plentiful, better endowed, and higher paying than those lost in the reshuffling. Manufacturing employment will decline, but industrial output will be diverted toward ever-higher-end technologies and products. In the meantime, just as investment shifted from agriculture to manufacturing, an increasing portion of capital and human resources will be redeployed in the service sector.

Analogies are comforting. They reduce our uncertainty about the future and provide the reassurance of "been there, done that." Unfortunately, analogies can also be misleading and this one is no exception. The shift from an agricultural to a manufacturing economy was the result of strong productivity gains anchored in technological improvements in machinery and fertilizers; it was not accelerated by trade competition because the world was not as globally integrated as it is today. The agricultural sector was (and, to a considerable extent, remains) protected, and logistics were less developed and more expensive. The reduction in agricultural employment did not result in the loss of production capacity and capabilities. Producers did not leave the country to grow their crops elsewhere, and workers (by-and-large) transited into higher-paying (though probably more alienating) jobs. While the shift to services is associated with productivity gains, it is also taking place in a relatively open global market with trade playing an important—though, by no means, exclusive—role. Displaced employees are driven, on average, to lower-paying jobs.

Although U.S. industrial output remains strong, there is no guarantee that it will be sustained into the future. The implications may be far reaching: "Experience has taught me that manufactures are now as necessary to our independence as to our comfort," wrote Thomas Jefferson in an 1816 letter to Benjamin Austin.[2] The words still ring true today and national security, while pivotal, may not be the only consideration. No less important is the possibility that the wholesale exit from mainline manufacturing activities will endanger (in the long range) the main competitive advantage of the U.S., namely its technological know-how and its ability to innovate. Already compromised by China's failure thus far to offer proper protection and compensation for intellectual property rights, erosion in technological capabilities will have ominous ramifications for the U.S. competitive position.

The Tortoise and the Hare

American advances in agricultural machinery were possible, among other reasons, because the country remained a major agricultural producer. This created demand and provided a testing ground for new inventions, many of which were later extended to industry. Today, the manufacturing sector fulfills the role of an innovation springboard and engine. According to the Institute of Electrical and Electronic Engineers (IEEE), manufacturing accounts for 62 percent of the research and development conducted in the U.S. (not to mention the bulk of its exports). Can such a feat be repeated when the agglomeration effect of multiple domestic competitors and supporting industries is gone? It is not clear that it can, and neither is it evident that the service sector can pick up the slack; after all, we have no precedent of a major economy that is predominantly dependent on services (the survival of Luxembourg, Hong Kong, and Hawaii as service economies—not without pain—can at least be partially attributed to their small size). It is also useful to recall that the forecasting record of economists, who promise us a replay of past patterns, isn't exactly stellar. The truth is, we are dealing with *terra incognita*.

In the same vein, it should not be taken for granted that it is possible to retain high-end manufacturing and research work at home while outsourcing other manufacturing activities. It is naïve to assume that China, or any other nation for that matter, will accept such a division of labor in the long run. In fact, all indications are that it won't. Exhibit 9-1 shows that while the U.S. high-technology exports have been on the increase, so have China's; the trend is likely to not only continue, but also accelerate. In fact, in the first quarter of 2004, China's high-tech exports were up more than 67 percent from a year earlier, according to China's Ministry of Commerce. While it is true that China-based foreign multinationals account for the bulk (75 to 85 percent, according to some estimates) of its high-tech exports and that much of the technology used by Chinese firms is not exactly leading-edge, the level of technology transfer to Chinese players—whether wittingly or not—is unprecedented. It would be imprudent to believe that China cannot eventually catch up with the West as it did over a millennium ago or as the U.S. did a century ago when it passed over the old world to become the world's leading economic power.

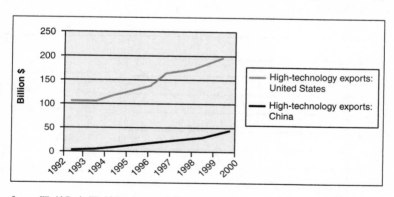

Source: World Bank, World Development Indicators, 2002.

Exhibit 9-1   High-Technology Exports of the U.S. and China.

China's R&D investment remains modest as a proportion of gross domestic product (GDP), though the growth in the Chinese economy means that the same proportion now buys much more. To compensate, China continues to provide preferences to foreign investment involving technology transfer and turns a blind eye to the free ride many of its firms enjoy as a result of lax intellectual property protection. Overall, as Exhibit 9-2 illustrates, China's payments for technology are very low but the numbers are skewed downward by technology transfer within multinational firms and by many Chinese producers avoiding payments for technology rights. Exhibit 9-2 also shows that though U.S. receipts for technology increased three fold from the 1980s to the 1990s, its technology payments have also been rising—a reminder that the nation does not have monopoly over new technology and innovation that some observers imply. The IEEE notes that China ranks second only to the U.S. in publishing technical papers in nanoscience and nanotechnology, and while the Chinese have been weak in bringing innovations to market, they are working hard on improving this handicap. Whether and how soon China will become a major innovation source remains to be seen, but it would be unwise to rule out the possibility. The country's firms have the ambition and determination and (increasingly) have the capital, human resources, and scale of operations to get them there.

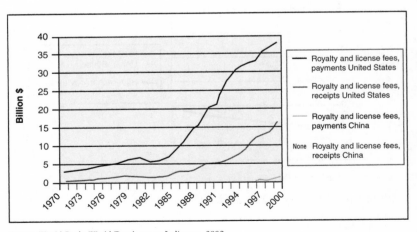

Source: World Bank, World Development Indicators, 2002.

Exhibit 9-2   Royalty and License Fee Payments and Receipts for the U.S. and China.

The video recorder, the industrial robot, and many other technological developments should remind us that invention and patenting do not guarantee commercial production, return on investment, or market dominance. Is the U.S. moving on to bigger and better things or is it simply giving away its technological edge by being overly transparent, selling too cheaply, transferring too easily, and allowing rampant copying without compensation or recourse? China is now receiving, copying, and assembling technology but it is clearly aiming at the most valuable type of know-how—the ability to create new knowledge and technology. In that, China is no different than Japan and the tigers, except that it has an historical record of innate innovation and that is building a formidable structure to do so. Surely, Britons were skeptical of the American ability to catch up with its know-how centuries ago; should we not consider the possibility that China will catch up with us one day?

China and the World Trade Organization

Many assessments on how China's impact will play out use the country's entry into the World Trade Organization (WTO) as an indicator of things to come. They see enhanced transparency, an open regulatory climate, and fortified protection of intellectual property rights augmenting opportunities for global exporters and investors in China's domestic market and otherwise leveling the playing field. Skeptics, in contrast, question whether the country will comply with the letter and spirit of its WTO accession agreements or rather find ways to avoid their full impact whenever perceived to be adverse to its domestic interests.

The record so far has been uneven. Side by side with considerable progress in some areas, violations—both fragrant and subtle—are abundant. A December 2003 report to Congress dedicated to China's WTO compliance asserted that while the country lived up to many of its WTO accession commitments, mostly in the areas of tariff reduction (for instance in chemicals, which resulted in a significant boost to U.S. exports), "in a number of different sectors, including some sectors of economic importance to the U.S., China fell far short of implementing its WTO commitments, offsetting many of the gains made in other areas...." The report goes on to cite agriculture, services, intellectual property rights, and transparency as problem areas already singled out in the 2002 report—all of which remain a concern today. The report concludes that, "China's uneven and incomplete WTO compliance record can no longer be attributed to start-up problems."[3]

The report paints a picture of systematic discrimination against foreign competitors. China is alleged to hand in subsidies to domestic producers who use them to lower prices in China as well as in global markets for goods ranging from machinery and petrochemicals to biomedicine. In other areas (such as semiconductors and fertilizers), value added tax (VAT) rebates are handed to domestic but not to foreign producers. On January 1, 2004, China reduced rebates on the exports of its domestic manufacturers (typically from 17 to 13 percent) but retained them for key lines such as automotive components. Many domestic producers pay much less since the declared value, which serves as a basis for the rebate, can be easily manipulated; others don't pay at all, benefiting from a chaotic environment or from protective local jurisdictions that are invested in the enterprise or are fearful of unemployment and unrest should local firms become less competitive.

Domestic players also receive preferences on consumption tax rates as well as on trading and distribution rights. WTO commitments regarding wholesaling services and commission agents' services provided by foreign firms were fulfilled to the extent that they relate to made-in-China products but not to imports. A variety of nontariff barriers (such as administrative guidance) keep foreign competitors out while the export of raw materials and intermediate products that support the competitiveness of domestic producers is curbed. China is also formulating unique standards in areas where international standards already exist, though it is certainly not the first country to do so. Foreign firms that wish to enter the Chinese retail sector face a myriad of regulatory approvals from which local players are exempt, and are denied majority control—except if they demonstrate, among other conditions, that they have purchased large amounts of Chinese goods.

Crucially, technology transfer continues to be used as a condition for investment approval or for the meting of incentives. China managed to escape an explicit clause banning all forms of such a tie-up when negotiating its WTO accession agreement, a risky concession on the part of foreign negotiators, though the link appears to be challenged in certain parts of the agreement. Many problems also continue in services, an area where the U.S. has a strong competitive advantage. All in all, this picture raises serious questions about the prospects of a sharp increase in U.S. exports to China at a pace sufficient to counterbalance projected growth in Chinese imports.

Scenarios for the Future

Forecasting the future is a tall task under any circumstances, and more so when the subject is a country of which it was once said: "The only thing certain about China is uncertainty." The subject of the China impact is complex and emotionally charged. It is multifaceted, involving multiple constituencies in different countries, with divergent interests, and whose actions cannot always be predicted. Future scenarios regarding the course of U.S.–China trade are hence difficult to draw, though it is possible to specify a range: from the optimistic soft landing, where China's trade surplus gradually declines as labor and material costs rise and the country fails to catch up with strong U.S. productivity and technology gains, to the less appealing scenario where an economically belligerent China—desperate to create jobs at home—encounters a rising protectionist sentiment in the U.S. and in other international markets, bringing the global economy down in the process.

Exhibit 9-3 shows alternative U.S.–China trade scenarios in 2008, calculated by the National Association of Manufacturers (NAM). The data show that if Chinese imports were to grow by 10 percent per year, a rather modest projection, the U.S. would need to increase exports by at least 25 percent annually in order to make a dent in the trade imbalance. This is not impossible: China is already the U.S.' fastest-growing export market and export growth in 2003 was well above that level. The question is whether that pace is sustainable given global competition and continuous preferences for domestic firms. Furthermore, even if U.S. exports were to sustain this rapid export pace, the growth of Chinese imports would have to fall to under 10 percent in order for the trade deficit to shrink; this too is unlikely. The NAM projections for 20 percent annual growth may be understated even under a currency revaluation scenario.

Import Growth	Export Growth 12%	Export Growth 25%	Export Growth 33%
20%	-$330	-$290	-$252
15%	-$246	-$205	-$167
10%	-$178	-$138	-$100
7%	-$144	-$104	-$66

Source: National Association of Manufacturers, 2003.

Exhibit 9-3 Projected Changes in U.S. Trade Deficits with China in 2008 (in Billions of U.S. Dollars): Alternative Scenarios.

Soft Landing

The soft-landing scenario is based on the predominant economic view of China as one more link in the natural evolution of international trade. Over time, Chinese wages will rise to a point where the country is no longer competitive in labor-intensive industries and thus vacate its position to Vietnam, Bangladesh, and others. China will channel more resources into its lagging service sector, relieving the intense pressure to attract more manufacturing capacity. The optimistic scenario calls for a gradual change in the exchange rate (there are signs that the Chinese government is considering this, to tame budding inflation, anyway) coupled with Chinese market-opening measures and a phase out of subsidies and other barriers that stack the cards against the foreign competitor. A real crackdown on piracy, motivated by both international pressure and Chinese interest in protecting domestic innovation, will restore the market share of U.S. and other country multinationals. In this scenario, China will also make a serious effort to buy American that—given the considerable power the government still holds—will lead to a rapid and sustained increase in U.S. exports focusing on big-ticket items such as aircraft. The trade deficit will shrink, alleviating protectionist pressures in a restructured U.S. economy that will produce more jobs.

There are a number of problems with the soft-landing scenario. It assumes that U.S. manufacturers in the low- and mid-technology segments will quickly climb to higher-end, high-technology production. The problem is that U.S. firms will not be the only ones trying to move up the ladder as a way of escaping vicious competition at the bottom. With other contenders—including China—vying for high value-added production, life at the top will get pretty crowded. The soft-landing scenario also assumes that the Chinese government will be willing and able to take on local interests that protect piracy and market manipulation, something the government has been reluctant to do in the past, and that the employment situation in China will stabilize to a point where export growth can be relaxed. It should also be noted that the soft-landing scenario, by definition, will play out over the long term. By the time it is consummated, China will have become much more efficient at directing capital and human resources and hence will have become a more formidable competitor.

Hard Landing

The hard-landing scenario sees a looming crisis between China and the U.S. that culminates in a clash with economic, political, and national security undercurrents. Pressured by continuous job losses in the manufacturing sector, the administration and/or Congress will undertake tariff or other protectionist measures—this time moving beyond WTO approved quotas on bras, robes, and knitted fabrics to cover such goods as automotive components, appliances, and other products with industry constituents who can muster enough political support. Union constituencies will continue to attack Chinese infringement of human rights but will invoke fair trade and reciprocity rather than protectionism. They may borrow a page from Tench Cox, who in a 1787 speech to the Pennsylvania Society for the Encouragement of Manufactures and Useful Arts said, "We must carefully examine the conduct of other countries in order to possess ourselves of their methods of encouraging manufactories and pursue such of them as apply to our situation, so far as it may be in our power."[4]

China will continue to defend its domestic industry, adding strong antidumping measures to its stable of subsidies and other market protections while continuing its strong defense of domestic players in trade disputes (China is known to transfer foreign filing information to domestic parties named in the complaint, providing them with judicial ammunition and commercial advantage). At the same time, it will mount aggressive defense toward antidumping investigations abroad. China will follow the U.S. (who was the first nation to appeal to the

WTO on a China-related matter) and launch its own appeals in the trade body. Case merits notwithstanding, the U.S. will not get much sympathy. Asia (which, as a whole, enjoys a considerable trade surplus with China) and Europe (which has a relatively small deficit) are unlikely to back an aggressive stand on Chinese violations. World public opinion may not help either: surprising to many Americans, many view the U.S. as the unfair trader. In a survey by Transparency International, a nonprofit, 58 percent of respondents ranked the U.S. government as most likely to use political pressure such as tied foreign aid to gain an unfair advantage in international markets. Number two, France, received only 26 percent. China ranked fifth, with only 16 percent of the sample believing it was using unfair advantage. Taiwan and Hong Kong received 5 and 1 percent, respectively.

Feeling increasingly isolated, the U.S. will turn inward, tuning to domestic currents rather than to international trade partners. From there, the situation may quickly deteriorate. Under increased pressure from unions and small manufacturers, the U.S. government will undertake unilateral measures (such as punitive tariffs) to protect its industry outside the WTO framework, threatening the global trade system. China will then dump its enormous dollar reserves, bringing about a dollar crash and a global financial meltdown.

Such a scenario is possible but unlikely. The report to Congress on China's WTO compliance notes that: "China has sought to deflect attention from its inadequate implementation of required systemic changes by managing trade in such a way as to temporarily increase affected imports from vocal trading partners, such as the U.S." Indeed, with the U.S. media and politicians increasingly criticizing China for its trade surplus in late 2003, the Chinese prepared a shopping mission to the U.S. but later scrapped it in reaction to the tariffs imposed on some apparel imports. To diffuse trade tensions, China will revalue the Yuan by a modest percentage—enough to placate the critics who have zeroed in on this issue, but hardly enough to make a difference in all but the most tightly contested product lines. Some Chinese firms will follow Haier and start U.S. manufacturing, but given wage and material cost differences, it will be a far cry from the scale of Japanese investment twenty-years ago.

A doomsday scenario is more likely to be triggered by internal Chinese problems that will then spill into the outside world. China faces a number of serious risks: Its financial system is close to insolvency and if the government were to lose its ability to prop it up, it could implode. A decline in the growth rate could send an already high unemployment rate into the stratosphere at a time when the social safety net is still nascent. Inequality between the coast and the hinterland and between the rich and the poor is growing by the day, which increases resentment and further erodes the fragile legitimacy of the Communist regime. In this environment, a trigger in the form of a steep and sudden revaluation could ignite social unrest and set off a violent reaction. A fall in domestic demand will then cause China to dump its enormous capacity in world markets and, given global overcapacity in many industries, the impact will be devastating. Foreign competitors will be pushed to sell at a loss, governments will set emergency tariffs, and exports will chase fewer and fewer open markets. The end result will be global depression on a scale not seen since the 1930s.

Fault Lines

A quarter of a century ago, U.S. car makers successfully lobbied the government to set "voluntary" quotas on Japanese-care imports. Today, this is unlikely to happen. The industries that are being hit hard (such as apparel and furniture) are much more fragmented, and many of their manufacturers and retailers are as dependent on Chinese inputs as the Chinese are on U.S. exports. Indeed, there is as much lobbying today to protect free trade (including Chinese imports and outsourcing) as to limit the flow of imports and outsourcing. The newly formed pro-trade Coalition for Economic Growth and American Jobs includes not only the expected Chamber of Commerce and trade groups, but also the National Association of Manufacturers. The coalition has set as its goal the defeat of legislation limiting outsourcing by U.S. government entities and is seeking to preserve the current number of work visas issued to foreign skilled employees. The U.S.–China Business Council, which includes some of the biggest exporters to China, has been also working hard to oppose any limitations on the flow of Chinese goods. With such strong internal support, it is no wonder China can afford to spend less than desolate Malawi on paid U.S. lobbyists.[5]

The battle lines drawn in the China debate may signal a permanent shift in the U.S. political landscape. Small manufacturers who are not adapt at outsourcing and lack global capabilities find themselves at odds with their big brothers who are relying on China for components and assembly. Unions are faced with more determined management who can threaten to walk away and offshore the operation, and will continue to lose ground as they rehash the old but ineffective China bashing on human rights. Individual voters find themselves embroiled in an internal conflict—their roles as employees, consumers, and shareholders stretch across the two sides of the debate: As consumers, they benefit from cheap Chinese products; as shareholders, they benefit from the profitability of China outsourcing; as employees, they are concerned with their jobs and with their ability to find new jobs in declining industries even if mitigated by the promise of renewed growth in a restructured economy.

Nations and States

In the U.S., states that are more dependent on China manufacturing are more likely to oppose limitations on China's exports, especially if they are not likely to lose many jobs as a result of Chinese imports. An example is the state of Washington, for whom China represents more than 11 percent of its total exports (see Exhibit 9-4) while its projected job losses from China trade (at about 7,000 according to the Economic Policy Institute) are among the lowest in the country. Southern states that are about to lose employment in mills and garment factories will see less benefit in an open trade with China, and so will Midwest states. China does not currently represent a big export market for the Midwest (except in agriculture), but employment losses from Chinese imports in the manufacturing sector—which are disproportionably represented there—are quite substantial. Hence, the China factor may create yet more schisms between the coasts and the hinterland, weaving it into the emerging political map. Similar phenomena will be observed in other countries where regions relying on labor-intensive or mid-technology industries find themselves on the opposite side of the table from those relying on agriculture or services who hope to benefit from the China trade.

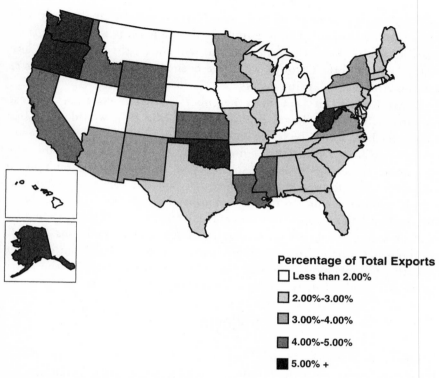

Exhibit 9-4 U.S. Exports to China, by State (2002).

Global Battle Lines

Outside the U.S., a crucial impact of China's rise will be the declining fortunes of the many developing economies that find it difficult to compete with China on exports and foreign investment. Nations that rely on labor-intensive industries (such as Egypt, Bangladesh, Sri Lanka, and many Central American and Caribbean countries), apparel in particular, will be especially hard hit since they have no substitute for those export industries. The result may be a sharper North–South divide, an ironic consequence given China's once championship of third-world causes. Pressured by Chinese competition in their most lucrative market, Latin American nations led by Mexico (which is seeing some of its hard won NAFTA benefits melt away) will press the U.S. to limit Chinese imports. These nations will invoke their traditional alliance of the Americas and will solicit the help of southern states such as North Carolina who have been the traditional suppliers to Central American clothing plants.

If Mexico and its southern neighbors were to continue to lose manufacturing jobs, illegal immigration to the U.S. would rise—but this time there would be fewer employment opportunities for the newly arrived. While agriculture, meatpacking, construction, and the restaurant trade will pick up some slack, it may not be enough to compensate for disappearing jobs in textile, apparel, carpet weaving, and simple manufacturing. In textile and apparel alone, the U.S. will likely lose at least half of its one-million current jobs, many of them staffed by first or second generation immigrants. Even agricultural jobs are not immune as Chinese produce exports grow (China is already an exporter of corn), though more jobs will likely be created at least in the short range as a result of increased agricultural exports to China.

Epilogue

Obstacles notwithstanding, the twenty-first century will see China restore its namesake as the Middle Kingdom. An industrial, commercial, and political hub, it will reach beyond East Asia—its traditional sphere of influence—first into Central and Southeast Asia and then into the world beyond, where it is destined to become one of two or three key players. It is only a matter of time (for instance) before China becomes closely involved in the Middle East, whose oil reserves it increasingly covets, or takes the lead in helping Africa out of its economic quagmire. Rather than being a guiding light for the "barbarians" surrounding it, China—this time around—will become a leading force in a competitive and interdependent world. As such, China may rewrite some of the same rules that other countries now expect it to abide by—whether on property rights or on international trade—challenging nations, firms, and individuals to adjust their business models and expectations. The massive movement of production factors that China is triggering may not only turn our economic theories and political assumptions on their head, but will also test fundamental threads in our society. How the coming challenge is handled will define much of the world our children will inherit.

Endnotes

Chapter 1

1 China's own numbers for the trade deficit with the U.S. are substantially lower, at about $70 billion for merchandise trade in 2002.

2 As described later in this book, Chinese apparel exports will pick up sharply in the coming years due to the expiration of the multifiber agreement and other factors.

3 N. R. Lardy, "United States-China Ties: Reassessing the Economic Relationship," Testimony before the House Committee on International Relations, U.S. House of Representatives, Washington D.C., 21 October 2003.

4 From instructions by Daniel Webster to Caleb Cushing, his emissary to China, whose mission resulted in the Treaty of Wanghia, signed on July 3, 1844. *Annals of American History.*

Chapter 2

1 K. Mazurewich, "With New Wealth, China's Tycoons Buy Lost Treasures," *The Wall Street Journal*, 14 January 2004: A1.

Chapter 3

1 Foreign investment figures for China are inflated by the inclusion of mainland companies who, in order to obtain incentives and overpass government restrictions, register in Hong Kong only to reinvest on the mainland (so-called "bogus blue eyed" ventures). However, the same is often true for foreign investment in other markets, as evidenced by the appearance of Luxembourg at the top of the UNCTAD foreign investment tables.

2 Huang, Yasheng, and Khanna, Tarun (2003), "Can India Overtake China?" *Foreign Policy*, July/August 2003.

3 Huang, Yasheng, and Khanna, Tarun (2003), "Can India Overtake China?" *Foreign Policy*, July/August 2003.

Chapter 4

1 Foreign Investment Administration, MOFTEC, 1998, "Tax Exemption Policies on Importation of Equipment by Enterprises with Foreign Investment," MOFTEC, Foreign Investment Administration. In *China in the World Economy*, OECD, 2002, Table 10-5.

2 United States Trade Representative, 2003 report to Congress on China WTO compliance, Washington D.C., December 11, 2003.

3 United States Trade Representative, 2003 report to Congress on China WTO compliance, Washington DC, December 11, 2003.

4 K. Kranhold, "Tough Bargain: China's Price for Market Entry: Give Us Your Technology, Too," *The Wall Street Journal*, 26 February 2004.

5 *China in the World Economy*, OECD, 2002.

6 P. J. Buckley, J. Clegg, and C. Wang, "The Impact of Inward FDI on the Performance of Chinese Manufacturing Firms," *Journal of International Business Studies*, vol. 33 no. 4 (2002): 637–655.

7 Zixiang (Alex) Tan, "Telecommunications, Technology, and China's Modernization," Paper presented at the conference on China-Europe Relations in Science and Technology, Rensselaer Polytechnic Institute, Troy, New York, September 4–6, 2003. To appear as a chapter in a forthcoming book, edited by Denis Simon and published by M.E. Sharpe.

8   *China in the World Economy*, OECD, 2002.

9   National Science Foundation (NSF), "U.S.-China R&D Linkages: Direct Investment and Industrial Alliances in the 1990s," NSF #306 (February 2004). Based on data from the Bureau of Economic Analysis.

10 United Nations Conference on Trade and Development (UNCTAD), Partnerships and networking in science and technology for development, Geneva, 2002.

11 National Science Foundation (NSF), "US-China R&D Linkages: Direct Investment and Industrial Alliances in the 1990s," NSF #306 (February 2004). Based on Thomson Financial Joint Venture/Alliance database.

12 The World Bank, World Development Indicators, 2002, Table 5.11.

13 *China in the World Economy*, OECD, 2002: 789.

14 Futao Huang, "Policy and Practices of the Internationalization of Higher Education in China," *Journal of Studies in International Education*, vol. 7 no. 3 (2003): 225–240.

15 C. Cao, "Brain Drain/Brain Gain/Brain Circulation and China's High-Level Human Resource Problem," Paper presented at the conference on China's Emerging Technological Trajectory in the 21st century, Rensselaer Polytechnic Institute, September 4–6, 2003. To be published as a chapter in a forthcoming book edited by Denis Simon and published by M.E. Sharpe.

16 J. M. Johnson, "Human Resource Contributions to U.S. Science and Engineering from China," NSF #311 (January 2001).

17 National Science Foundation, Division of Science Resources Statistics, *Survey of Earned Doctorates*, 2002.

18 J. M. Johnson and M.C. Regets, "International Mobility of Scientists and Engineers to the United States—Brain Drain or Brain Circulation?" NSF #316 (June 1998).

19 C. Cao, "Brain Drain/Brain Gain/Brain Circulation and China's High-Level Human Resource Problem," Paper presented at the conference on China's Emerging Technological Trajectory in the 21st century, Rensselaer Polytechnic Institute, September 4–6, 2003. To be published as a chapter in a forthcoming book edited by Denis Simon and published by M.E. Sharpe.

20 H. Choi, *An International Scientific Community—Asian Scholars in the United States*. (New York: Praeger, 1995).

21 J. Sigurdson, "China-Europe Relations in Science and Technology," Paper presented at the conference on China's Emerging Technological Trajectory in the 21st century, Rensselaer Polytechnic Institute, Troy, New York, September 4–6, 2003. To appear as a chapter in a forthcoming book, edited by Denis Simon and published by M.E. Sharpe.

22 D. F. Simon, "China's High-Tech Thrust: Beijing's Evolving Approaches to the Process of Innovation," *China Economic Review*, vol. 1 no. 1 (1989): 73–92.

23 MOST 1999, Cited in OECD, 2002: 202.

24   *China in the World Economy*, OECD, 2002: 206.

25   Yifei Sun and Hongyang Wang, "Technological Innovation in Rural Enterprises of Jiangsu, China," Paper presented at the conference on China's Emerging Technological Trajectory in the 21st century, Rensselaer Polytechnic Institute, September 4–6, 2003. To be published as a chapter in a forthcoming book edited by Denis Simon and published by M.E. Sharpe.

Chapter 5

1   Development Research Center, China's State Council, reported in *The China Business Review*, 6 December 2003; United States Trade Representative, 2003 report to Congress on China's WTO compliance, Washington, D.C., 11 December, 2003.

2   International Intellectual Property Alliance (IIPA), public comment on the identification of countries under Section 182 of the Trade Act of 1974 to the Office of the United States Trade Representative. Washington, D.C., February 13, 2004.

3   Daniel C. K. Chow, "Counterfeiting in the People's Republic of China," *Washington University Law Quarterly*, vol. 78 no. 1 (2000): 1–57.

4   Kitty McKinsey, "Watching for Chinese Knock-Offs," *Electronic Business*, 1 January 2003: 2–6; International Intellectual Property Alliance, 2003 Special 301 Report, People's Republic of China.

5   *Business Week*, 5 June 2002.

6   United States Trade Representative, 2003 report to congress on China's WTO compliance, Washington, D.C., 11 December 2003.

7   International Intellectual Property Alliance, *2003 Special 301 Report*, People's Republic of China.

8   *Time*, 11 June 2001: 35.

9   International Intellectual Property Alliance, *2003 Special 301 Report*, People's Republic of China.

10   United States Trade Representative, 2003 report to Congress on China WTO compliance, Washington, D.C. December 11, 2003.

11   Kitty McKinsey, "Watching for Chinese Knock-Offs," *Electronic Business*, 1 January 2003: 3.

12   "Busting Software Pirates," *Time Europe*, November 18, 2002, Cited in International Intellectual Property Alliance (IIPA), Public Comment on the Identification of Countries under Section 182 of the Trade Act of 1974 to the Office of the United States Trade Representative, Washington, D.C., February 13, 2004.

13   R. Buckman, "Blockbuster to Close All Stores in Hong Kong by Mid-2005," *The Wall Street Journal*, February 2, 2004: B3.

14   G. A. Fowler, "Universal's China Business Plan Tries to Neutralize Music Piracy," *The Wall Street Journal*, February 27, 2004: B5.

Chapter 6

1   Ira Kalish, "The World's Factory: China Enters the 21st Century," *Deloitte Research*, 2003.

2   "A Survey of Business in China," *The Economist*, March 20, 2004.

3   U.S. Department of Commerce, Special report to the Congressional Textile Caucus on the administration's efforts on textile issues, December 2003.

4   F. Zhai and S. Li, "Quantitative Analysis and Evaluation of Entry to WTO on China's Economy," *China Development Review* 3 no. 2 (2001), Development Research Center of the State Council, People's Republic of China.

5   Y. Yang, "China's Integration into the World Economy: Implications for Developing Countries," International Monetary Fund Working Paper, WP/03/245, 2003.

6   Christopher Rhoads, "China Threat Fashions a Period of Upheaval for Italy's Textile Firms," *The Asian Wall Street Journal*, 17 December 2002: A1.

7   Dan Morse, "Furniture Makers Seek Trade Duties," *The Wall Street Journal*, 3 November 2002: A2.

8   "Furniture Makers Seek Trade Sanctions, CNN Money, 1 November 2003.

9   "Furniture Makers Seek Trade Sanctions, CNN Money, 1 November 2003.

10 D. Morse, "In North Carolina, Furniture Makers Try to Stay Alive," *The Wall Street Journal*, February 20, 2004: A1; A. Higgins, "As China Surges, It Also Proves a Buttress to American Strength." *The Wall Street Journal*, January 30, 2004: A1.

11 "The Sucking Sound from the East," *The Economist*, 26 July 2003: 36.

12 R. Watkins, "Mexico Versus China: Factors Affecting Export and Investment Competition," *Industry Trade and Technology Review*, July 2002.

13 Division of Trade Statistics, International Monetary Fund, cited in W.M. Cox and J. Koo, "China: Awakening Giant," Federal Reserve Bank of Dallas, September 2003.

14 W. Michael Cox and Jahyeong Koo, "China: Awakening Giant," Federal Reserve Bank of Dallas, September 2003.

15 Juan Forero, "As China Gallops, Mexico Sees Factory Jobs Slip Away," *The Wall Street Journal*, 3 September 2003: A3.

16 R. Watkins, "Mexico Versus China: Factors Affecting Export and Investment Competition," *Industry Trade and Technology Review*, July 2002.

17 Barbara Kastelein, "Mexico Balks at Growing China 'Invasion,'" *Plastics News*, vol. 15 no. 4 (24 March 2003).

18 F. Salim, Presentation at the Institute for International Research in San Diego, CA, March 19, 2002, based on a GE study. Cited in R. Watkins, "Mexico Versus China: Factors Affecting Export and Investment Competition," *Industry Trade and Technology Review*, July 2002.

19   Ira Kalish, "The World's Factory: China Enters the 21st Century," *Deloitte Research*, 2003.

20   Joseph B. White, "Unglamorous Axle Maker Is As Good As Gold," *The Wall Street Journal*, 10 November 2003: B1.

21   S. Diesenhouse, "To Save Factories, Owners Diversify," *The New York Times*, 30 November 2002: 5.

22   Melissa Fowler, "Manufacturer Uses Chinese-Made Products to Grow, *Dayton Business Journal*, 4 August 2003.

23   D. Morse, "In North Carolina, Furniture Makers Try to Stay Alive," *The Wall Street Journal*, February 20, 2004: A1.

24   The Nippert information has been provided by Chris Nippert, a former executive of the firm and a son of the founder.

25   E. Ramstad, "Flat-Panel, Plasma TV Sets Bring a Flood of New Brands," *The Wall Street Journal*, January 13, 2004: B1.

Chapter 7

1   Kletzer, Lori, "Job Loss from Imports: Measuring the Costs." Washington DC: Institute for International Economics, 2001.

2   Ashok D. Bardhan and Cynthia Kroll, "The New Wave of Outsourcing." Fisher Center for Real Estate and Urban Economics, #1103 University of California, Berkeley, 2003.

3   "New Opponents of Free Trade," *The Wall Street Journal*, 10 October 2003.

4   Ashok D. Bardhan and Cynthia Kroll, "The New Wave of Outsourcing." Fisher Center for Real Estate and Urban Economics, #1103 University of California, Berkeley, 2003.

5   "Job Migration: Is It a Win-Win Game?" McKinsey Global Institute, McKinsey & Company, 2003. The numbers include a high portion of software and other high-tech works, so tiny Israel, for instance, is a destiny for $3 billion in offshored work.

6   Honeck, J., "International Trade and Job Loss in Ohio," Policy Matters Ohio, February 2004.

7   Ashok D. Bardhan and Cynthia Kroll, "The New Wave of Outsourcing," Fisher Center for Real Estate and Urban Economics, #1103 University of California, Berkeley, 2003.

8   Hilsenrath, J.E., "Behind Outsourcing Debate: Surprisingly Few Hard Numbers," *The Wall Street Journal*, April 12, 2004, A1.

9   Hira, Ron, Testimony on behalf of the IEEE to the Committee on Small Business. U.S. House of Representatives, 18 June 2003.

10 "Job Migration: Is It a Win-Win Game?" McKinsey Global Institute, McKinsey & Company, 2003.

11 The Federal Reserve Bank of Chicago cites a figure of only 13 percent of the sales of China-based U.S. multinationals being shipped back to the United States; it acknowledges that contracts of such affiliates with China-owned plants are not included in the count. See Midwest manufacturing and trade with China, Chicago Fed Letter, The Federal Reserve Bank of Chicago, Essays on Issues #196, November 2003. In addition, with overall sales of China-based affiliates growing, the same percentage will yield more U.S. imports.

12 There are reasons to believe that this number is understated because of the difficulty of measuring virtual offshoring and the negative political atmosphere surrounding the practice.

13 Forrester Research; "Job Migration: Is It a Win-Win Game?" McKinsey Global Institute, McKinsey & Company, 2003.

14 Scott, Robert E., "Fast Track to Lost Jobs." The Economic Policy Institute. October 2001.

15 Kletzer, Lori, "Job Loss from Imports: Measuring the Costs." Washington DC: Institute for International Economics. See also "Trade Balance: Tipping Scales to Add Workers." *The Wall Street Journal*, 30 August 2001: A1.

16 "Job Migration: Is It a Win-Win Game?" McKinsey Global Institute, McKinsey & Company, 2003.

17 OECD, 1999 Employment Report, chapter 2.

18 Bulkeley, Willliam M., "IBM Documents Give Rare Look at 'Offshoring,'" *The Wall Street Journal*, 19 January 2004: A1.

19 Budman, Matthew, "Looking Ahead to Our Place in the Next Economy," *Across the Board*, 16.

20 Colvin, Jeffrey, "Value Driven," *Fortune.* 27 October 2003. Jon E. Hilsenrath and Rebecca Buckman, "Factory Employment Is Falling Worldwide," *The Wall Street Journal*, 20 October 2003: A2.

21 Groshen, Erica L. and Potter, Simon, "Has Structural Change Contributed to a Jobless Recovery?" *Current Issues in Economics and Finance,* vol. 9 no. 8 (2004). See also Federal Reserve Bank of New York, August 2003. Interview with Erica Groshen in January, 2004.

22 "U.S. Job Losses 'Not China's Fault,'" *The Standard* (Hong Kong), 6 December 2003: A4.

23 "U.S. Blames Job Loss on China," *CNN.com*, 8 January 2004.

24 Bjorhus, Jennifer, "The Tradeoff of Trade with China: Jobs," *Twin Cities.com*, Pioneer Press, 27 April 2003.

25 "Where Free Trade Hurts," *Business Week*, 15 December, 2003.

26 Kletzer, Lori, and Litan, Robert, "A Prescription to Relieve Workers' Anxiety," *Policy Brief* 01-2, IIE, February 2001.

27 Denlinger, Paul, *China Business Strategy*, 4 September 2003.

28 "Offshore, Onshore," *The Wall Street Journal*, February 26, 2004: B4.

29 Fisher, A., "Where the Jobs Are Now and How to Get Them," *Fortune.com*, March 16, 2004.

30 Gongloff, M., "Is the Job Market Broken?" *CNNmoney*, February 9, 2004.

Chapter 8

1 Zeynep Gurhan-Canli and Durairaj Maheswaran, "Cultural Variations in Country of Origin Effects, *Journal of Marketing Research*, July 2000: 309.

2 Tracie Rozhon, "Decking the Stores with No-Name Brands, *International Herald Tribune*, 11 December 2003: 14.

3 International Trade Commission, "Wooden Bedroom Furniture from China." Investigation No. 731-TA-1058 (Preliminary), Publication 3667, Washington, D.C. January 2004.

4 Jill Gabrielle Klein, Richard Ettenson, and Marlene D. Morris, "The Animosity Model of Foreign Product Purchase: An Empirical Test in the People's Republic of China," *Journal of Marketing*, vol. 62 no. 1: 89.

5 Gary S. Insch, "The Impact of Country-of-Origin Effects on Industrial Buyers' Perceptions of Product Quality," *Management International Review*, vol. 43 no. 3 (2003): 291–310.

6 "The Last Sector Where Made in Europe Matters," *Financial Times*, 4 December 2003: 16.

7 Dana Frank, *Buy American: The Untold Story of Economic Nationalism* (Boston: Beacon Press, 1999), 131–213.

8 Michael Forsythe, "Wal-Mart's China Goods Fuel U.S. Suppliers' Anger," *International Herald Tribune*, 8 July 2003.

Chapter 9

1 Reich, Robert B., "Nice Work If You Can Get It," *The Wall Street Journal*, 26 December 2003.

2 Jefferson, Thomas, "On the Present Need to Promote Manufacturers," Memoirs, Correspondence, and Private Papers of Thomas Jefferson, 1829, *Annals of American History*, vol. IV, 276-279.

3 United States Trade Representative, 2003 report to Congress on China's WTO compliance, Washington, D.C., 11 December 2003.

4 Cox, Tench, "Prospects for American Manufacturers," A View of the United States of America, etc., etc., Philadelphia, 1794, *Annals of American History*, 35-36.

5 Basken, P. and Forsythe, M., "China's Powerful Friends in High Places," *The Japan Times*, Sec. 12, 2003: 19.

Index

The Fortune at the Bottom of the Pyramid

The world's most exciting, fastest-growing new market? It's where you least expect it: *at the bottom of the pyramid*. Collectively, the world's billions of poor people have immense entrepreneurial capabilities and buying power. You can learn how to serve them and help millions of the world's poorest people escape poverty.

It is being done—*profitably*. Whether you're a business leader or an anti-poverty activist, business guru Prahalad shows why you can't afford to ignore "Bottom of the Pyramid" (BOP) markets.

ISBN 0131467506, © 2005, 432 pp., $28.95

The Power of Impossible Thinking

You don't live in the real world. You live in the world inside your head. We all do. Our invisible mental models shape everything we do. Often, they keep us from seeing what's right in front of us, and prevent us from changing our companies and society... even our *lives*. *The Power of Impossible Thinking* is about fixing your mental models, so you can *see* reality and *act* on it. Based firmly in neuroscience, it shows how to develop new ways of seeing... understand complex environments... even how to do "mind R&D" to keep your models fresh and relevant. Whether you need to beat the competition or lose weight, your mental models may be the problem... and *The Power of Impossible Thinking* is the solution.

ISBN 0131425021, © 2005, 336 pp., $24.95

The Wharton School of the

"Great schools have…endeavored to do more than keep up to the respectable standard of a recent past; they have labored to supply the needs of an advancing and exacting world…"

— **Joseph Wharton,** *Entrepreneur and Founder of the Wharton School*

The Wharton School is recognized around the world for its innovative leadership and broad academic strengths across every major discipline and at every level of business education. It is one of four undergraduate and 12 graduate and professional schools of the University of Pennsylvania. Founded in 1881 as the nation's first collegiate business school, Wharton is dedicated to creating the highest value and impact on the practice of business and management worldwide through intellectual leadership and innovation in teaching, research, publishing and service.

Wharton's tradition of innovation includes many firsts—the first business textbooks, the first research center, the MBA in health care management—and continues to innovate with new programs, new learning approaches, and new initiatives. Today Wharton is an interconnected community of students, faculty, and alumni who are shaping global business education, practice, and policy.

Wharton is located in the center of the University of Pennsylvania (Penn) in Philadelphia, the fifth-largest city in the United States. Students and faculty enjoy some of the world's most technologically advanced academic facilities. In the midst of Penn's tree-lined, 269-acre urban campus, Wharton students have access to the full resources of an Ivy League university, including libraries, museums, galleries, athletic facilities, and performance halls. In recent years, Wharton has expanded access to its management education with the addition of Wharton West, a San Francisco academic center, and The Alliance with INSEAD in France, creating a global network.

Wharton
UNIVERSITY *of* PENNSYLVANIA

Academic Programs:

Wharton continues to pioneer innovations in education across its leading undergraduate, MBA, executive MBA, doctoral, and executive education programs.

More information about Wharton's academic programs can be found at:
http://www.wharton.upenn.edu/academics

Executive Education:

Wharton Executive Education is committed to offering programs that equip executives with the tools and skills to compete, and meet the challenges inherent in today's corporate environment. With a mix of more than 200 programs, including both open enrollment and custom offerings, a world-class faculty, and educational facilities second to none, Wharton offers leading-edge solutions to close to 10,000 executives annually, worldwide.

For more information and a complete program listing:
execed@wharton.upenn.edu (sub 4033)
215.898.1776 or 800.255.3932 ext. 4033
http://execed.wharton.upenn.edu

Research and Analysis:

Knowledge@Wharton is a unique, free resource that offers the best of business—the latest trends; the latest research on a vast range of business issues; original insights of Wharton faculty; studies, paper and analyses of hundreds of topics and industries. *Knowledge@Wharton* has over 400,000 users from more than 189 countries.

For free subscription:
http://knowledge.wharton.upenn.edu

For licensing and content information, please contact:
Jamie Hammond,
Associate Marketing Director,
hammondj@wharton.upenn.edu • 215.898.2388

Wharton School Publishing:

Wharton School Publishing is an innovative new player in global publishing, dedicated to providing thoughtful business readers access to practical knowledge and actionable ideas that add impact and value to their professional lives. All titles are approved by a Wharton senior faculty review board to ensure they are relevant, timely, important, empirically based and/or conceptually sound, and implementable

For author inquiries or information about corporate education and affinity programs or, please contact:
Barbara Gydé, Managing Director,
gydeb@wharton.upenn.edu • 215.898.4764

The Wharton School: http://www.wharton.upenn.edu
Executive Education: http://execed.wharton.upenn.edu
Wharton School Publishing: http://whartonsp.com
Knowledge@Wharton: http://knowledge.wharton.upenn.edu